Radiantly Free

Re-creating Life & Health
From the Radiance of You

Rev. Dr. Rachel Wetzsteon

Edited by Connie Anderson & Jean Wetzsteon

ISBN 13: 978-0-9997084-0-8
eISBN 13: 978-0-9997084-1-5

Library of Congress Control Number: 2017918667

Rev. Dr. Rachel Wetzsteon
Rachel Wetzsteon PhD
Lakeville, Minnesota
www.drrachelw.com

I dedicate this book to the loves of my life.
Kanen and Weston - my boys - thank you for your
unconditional love and for how you have helped
me grow and see life in a new way.
Allan - my husband - thank you for your friendship
and support on this journey.
Mom and Dad - Jean and Bob - I'm so glad we
chose each other. Thank you for this life and your
love.

Table of Contents

Introduction

Radiantly Free is a book about healing and fully living our greatest potential in health and happiness. Several years ago I went through a dramatic shift in my life. I had been living in overwhelm, stress, and fatigue. And while my life didn't look that way from the outside, on the inside I was simply going through the motions and trying to get through the day. I could put a nice smile on my face and enjoy some moments, but I wasn't feeling joyful, light, and free on the inside.

I remember waking up one morning, feeling heavy and tired as usual. I thought about how I had achieved or created everything I had ever wanted, including having two beautiful boys, a great husband, my doctoral degree, a beautiful home, and a sweet dog. I wondered, why the heck don't I wake up joyful and happy about the day and my life?

I knew I needed to take a look at what was going on inside of me. A part of me knew it wasn't about the busy-ness of having children, the daily grind, or that I sometimes felt irritated with other people. I knew I had to own my emotions, learn about what was going on inside of me, and figure me out.

Fortunately, great opportunities for learning and growth came across my path. I began attending a spirituality center that taught me to change my thinking. I began a meditation practice, and I found a renewed passion for reading. I had loved to read in my childhood; however, over the years, reading academic textbooks and research articles had drained me. I reached a point where I couldn't even bring myself to read another research article. I feel that God, Life, the Universe, or whatever you want to call IT, was helping me move in another direction. Thank Go(o)dness for that!! Over a period of about six months I read about 40 books having to do with personal and spiritual growth, energy healing, awareness for transcending charged emotions, how our experience of God changes our physiology, and so on. I found myself, and I felt so alive and excited about life again. I had finally truly found my passion.

I came to understand that I had not been living from my God-self, that is, the eternal part of you and me that never dies and is always free. The solution to our problems is that simple, yet there is some growth to do once we realize that *is our Truest potential.* We have built up defenses, conditioning, and patterns that we have created up until this point in our life, and this shows up in our energy field - and thus, in our body. Once we realize this is not where our happiness is, then we can begin the process of becoming aware and begin dumping all of our "stuff" that does not align with our radiant freedom.

With a doctoral degree in exercise physiology and having taught group fitness classes for 18 years, I knew all of the rules and guidelines when it came to the human body. Unfortunately, the focus in the medical and fitness fields is restricted to medicine, diet, and exercise. Through the awakening I experienced, I became attuned to the energetic, mental, and emotional aspects of ourselves that contribute to the wellness of our bodies and our potential to live radiantly free. This is an internal experience and the more we shift and heal our emotions and our mind, as well as create shifts in our perceptions, our external experience of life also changes.

Our Radiance is a product of the clarity of our personal bioenergy field and the clarity and presence of the mind. I invite you to join me on a journey of living *Radiantly Free*.

Chapter 1: The Meaning of Radiantly Free

Radiantly Free represents the radiance of our bioenergy field and the liberation of the mind. Our emotions, thoughts, beliefs, and conditioning are all bound up in our energy field, and most humans have a quite dense energetic body. Everything is energy and everything has a vibration. The denser the energy, the lower the vibration. The lighter and more open the energy, the higher and faster the vibration.

The objective in becoming Radiantly Free is to release all that is inhibiting or blocking our energy from flowing freely and our mind from living joyfully in the present moment. We can free ourselves from the non-stop mental chatter, ruminating, and over-analyzing and open to insight and intuition. Another important component to healing is the lessening of the charge of strong emotional reactions. The more the charge of our strong negative emotions lessen, the more joy and love we are able to radiate. Becoming lighter energetically is a path of awareness, observing, breathing, and healing. It is about letting go of whatever is up for us, and letting go of making it about anyone or anything else. Our emotions, reactions, and drama are ours and only we have the power to heal it and to free ourselves.

Being Radiantly Free feels like joy, bliss, lightness, love, being, inspiration, guidance, connection, aliveness, laughter, peace, and acceptance.

In living our Godly potential, the perception of life is in wonder, awe, and miracles. There is an appreciation and delight for nature, for beauty felt in everything and everyone, and for a sense of how fabulous it is that we are even here at all - being held on earth by gravity and moving perfectly on orbit through space. Do you feel what an absolute miracle that is?

When we are living lightly, free from creating drama, our natural tendency is to see the Go(o)d in people. Some humans have a habit of focusing on what they don't like instead of what they do like. The people who show up in our lives reflect us, so whatever we notice that we dislike in someone else is an opportunity to ask ourselves, "Where is this in me?" We heal our relationships when we take full responsibility for ourselves, and how we show up.

In living Radiantly Free, the perception of life is not that everything happens by chance or randomly, but that there is Divine perfection and alignment in everything, and all things line up and occur in a perfect Diving timing. This is easy to sense when things are going great, but what if you felt this even when things weren't going well. There truly is perfection in what appears as imperfection. Energetically, life is perfectly reflecting us, and we attract what we are - life reflects us like a mirror.

Our potential is to be the peaceful observer and to let Life live through us freely and lightly.

What we experience in our daily life is the result of what we have co-created with Life, God, the Universe, whatever you want to call IT. No one, not even God, is handing anything to us. When we start living more and more in the present moment, we take more notice of the world around us. We can experience life in an enchanted way. Life, God, the Universe, whatever you want to call IT, gives us signs that we are on the right track. This may show up as noticing regular repeating times on the clock, such as 11:11, 1:11, 4:44, 12:34, etc., the numbers of your total at the store checkout, and various words or symbols on signs or license plates. We feel connected to nature and take notice of the animals that appear in our life. Because of this connected and guided feeling, all doubt, fear, and uncertainty eventually diminish and we experience True Faith and knowing.

Another sign of being Radiantly Free is a willingness to check all of our beliefs and question whether each one is really what we want to create for ourselves. We can only experience life or God to the extent that we are open to it. Open mindedness is a significant component to being open to experiences and shifts in our beliefs. If we are very rigid in what we believe God to be, rigid in what we believe about our body, or stuck in what we believe our capabilities are, for instance, then we will experience and create only what we are attached to creating with our limited concepts of life. There is a lighter, more intuitive, trusting, open, and joyful way to be and live in the world.

When our life energy is free from our conditioning, we have shifts in perception, such as shifting from self-hatred to self-love, from struggle to ease, from victim to creator, closed mindedness to open mindedness, and from problems to potential. There are changes in our brain physiology that correlate with these shifts in perception. We get out of lower brain fear-based negativity, problems, and worry and we shift into, generally speaking, higher-brain confidence, authenticity, inner-peace, insight, and intuition. Yes, there are proven research-based changes that happen in our brain and body when we get out of the lower brain stress response - we find God and we know our relationship to God as *one with it*. We have a Divine spark within us, each and every one of us, and we can gently nudge it into a sacred fire of radiant life energy.

Interestingly, becoming unconditionally loving is made possible by a physiological and energetic occurrence. Our energy field must be significantly cleared out, and we cannot be operating from lower-brain dominance. To truly be a loving presence fully radiating the Love of Life, we have to free up the energy and control of the lower-brain and get into a higher-brain perceiving dominance. Dr. Michael Cotton, one of my favorite teachers on evolutionary brain changes and thriving in life and the creator and founder of Higher Brain Living, says that the heart cannot fully open until we get out of the stress of the lower-brain.

Prior to the start of my healing and spiritual journey, I had intuitive experiences for which I didn't have words. I didn't grow up with anyone teaching me about intuition; however, in retrospect I see and understand what I was "getting." Now, I often feel a gushing of energy through the heart area of my body. Let's go into more about the human bioenergy field.

Our human bodies emanate from our human energy field. This energy field of the heart can be measured with equipment up to 15 feet away from an individual, however people report having experienced themselves as "infinite" and that is what the saints and sages also tell us. I have felt this sense that we are infinitely in and infinitely out. Some people are able to see energy fields or auras around people and this ability is called "clairvoyance." Sometimes people use the word "aura" to describe what they are able to see or sense, however the energy of our being is quite intricate and more complex than what we see in an aura image that is taken with an imaging device. There are layers and dimensions to our bioenergy field. Please see the book, *Hands of Light: A Guide to Healing Through the Human Energy Field*, by Barbara Ann Brennan, for an in-depth study of the human energy field. The aspects of our energy field that I do want to cover are the energy areas that are called "chakras." These were first discussed in The Vedas, which are among the oldest sacred texts.

We have seven major chakra energy centers that are a primary component of the human bioenergy field. My first experience with chakras occurred when I was attending a group fitness class, and the instructor mentioned our chakras as we were sitting cross legged on the floor. I had never heard this word before so I asked her, "What are chakras?" She responded, "They are energy centers." They came up again as I was reading a book one evening. It described an exercise to tune into the energy of the body, and I noticed I could not feel this energy in some places in my body.

I called the instructor friend who had mentioned the chakras in her class and I told her that I couldn't feel my energy in various areas of my body. She told me that I was blocked, so as soon as I could, I went to see her to find out more and to get unblocked. This was the start of my energy healing path. I discovered that two of my chakras were closed: my root chakra and my throat chakra. This didn't surprise me because I have often held back in speaking up or in speaking my truth. I grew up uncomfortably shy, and I did want to feel some liberation in my ability to communicate. I also found out that my root chakra was closed because I did not feel safe and supported in the world. It became my mission to open these chakras, and become as clear as I could be so I could radiate and help move energy for other people in their own healing of their energy field. Here is a brief description of the seven primary chakra energy centers:

The base or first chakra is called the root chakra. The color of this energy center is red. The root chakra has to do with feeling safe, supported, and secure in the world. It is our energy center related to our ability to trust Life, create abundance, and feel at home in ourselves and wherever we are in the world.

The second energy center is called the sacral chakra. The color of this energy center is orange. The sacral chakra is associated with our openness to creativity, sexuality, and playfulness.

The third energy center is called the solar plexus chakra. The color of this energy center is yellow. The solar plexus chakra is where we feel our sense of power and it is a significant energy center in the balance of give and receive in relationships. The solar plexus chakra also needs a balance of our creating boundaries and honoring other people's boundaries.

The fourth energy center is called the heart chakra. The color of the heart chakra is green. This energy center is where we are open or closed to Love and when this center is radiantly open, we feel unconditional Love for all of life. This isn't about emotional and attached love of other people. That would actually be a block to true Love. True Love doesn't need someone and a person's value isn't determined by the love or lack of love from another person. "Having an open heart" isn't just a statement about a kind person. There is an energetic opening that must happen to truly have an open heart.

True Love doesn't dislike itself,
hate any other people, criticize,
or create a drama-filled life.
True Love is defenseless and unattached.

The fifth energy center is called the throat chakra, and its color is blue. This is the energy center where we communicate Truth, speak when we are guided to speak, and stay silent when it is time for silence.

The sixth energy center is called the third eye chakra. The color of this chakra is indigo. An open third eye chakra gives us insight, intuition, clarity, and the ability to choose peace of mind.

The seventh energy center is called the crown chakra. The color of the crown chakra is purple/ violet. When the crown chakra is open we feel connected to Life, God, the Universe, whatever you want to call IT, and feel a general contentment and ease with the world. The crown chakra is also about feeling connected to nature and feeling alive and well.

Our chakras are also associated with certain organs of the body, so if there is a health issue with a certain organ we would look to the corresponding chakra and life pattern that is creating disruption in the energy field. I would like to emphasize that understanding your chakras and where you might be having blockages is just one aspect of our complex being. Some people can sense the open or closed status of each of the chakras, and you can have them checked by an individual trained to use a pendulum. The pendulum is held over the area of each chakra. If the pendulum is still, then the chakra is closed. The pendulum might move in circular or elliptical patterns and ideally, the pattern would be circular and clockwise if the chakra is open and flowing. The energy blockages represent the energy of traumas, emotional pain, and our mental constructs, and these blockages prevent our life energy from flowing freely. When the energy blockages persist over time they affect the body and may eventually lead to dis-ease, pain, and mental disorder. Healing, rejuvenation, and joy happen when we clear out the "stuff" that is preventing us from living *Radiantly Free*.

We can get an idea of where we are blocked by where we "protect" ourselves. Notice if you cross your arms over your solar plexus area. You may be protecting yourself from being disempowered by others. Do you protect your root chakra by clasping your hands down low with your arms straight? I have seen people who cross their arms over their heart or hold their hand in front of their throat. Start to take notice of this in yourself and in others.

We can live from the radiance of our God-self when our energy is clear and light or we can live from all that is not that. Throughout the book you will notice I use dis-ease instead of disease. The medical field has mistaken disease for something that needs a medication, however dis-ease is really a mis-alignment with our God-self. And dis-ease will feel exactly that - it will feel like a struggle instead of ease. There is a bit of digging and self awareness that needs to go into clearing and shifting our energy into alignment with who we really are. I will share a personal story about being prescribed a medication I really did not need.

When I was in my early twenties, I had an appointment with an internal medicine doctor. I was there for a routine wellness visit, but I asked her about anti-depressants. I was feeling what one might call "depressed", and I lacked direction and didn't have inspired motivation. I cried a little, and she was very quick to prescribe me an anti-depressant without any questions and without a referral to anyone to talk to about my concerns. Honestly, at that age I probably didn't want to talk to anyone - I was okay with the quick fix of a pill.

As I have reflected back on this period of my life, I certainly should not have been on an anti-depressant. It doesn't mix well with alcohol, and alcohol is a part of the life of many 21 year olds. Alcohol is a depressant, and perhaps I would have been much happier and clearer on my path without it. But, I now know I was not depressed, but I was simply not living from my God-self. Moreover, I did not know that living Radiantly Free was an option. It is. Thank Go(o)dness for awakening.

After reading this chapter, do you have a sense of something moving in you? Did you have an awareness about yourself? Or do you sense a way to see life or the events of your life in a new way? Let's go deeper together… continue to Chapter 2 - Free the Godly You.

Chapter 2: Free the Godly You

Living from the freedom of the Godly You starts with a peeling back or an opening of all of the layers we have built up around ourselves that block our freest, lightest expression. Energetically, the vibration of the Soul is very fast, and this high-frequency vibration translates to emotions of predominantly joy, unconditional Love, compassion, gratitude, and bliss. When we are feeling fear, overwhelm, stress, worry, anger, and angst, we are in a low vibration. We all have a personal vibration set-point or where we are vibrating most of time - and we can be at different vibrations throughout the day. How we are vibrating also determines how the body is functioning. When the Godly You is freely expressed, the body is flexible and moving joyfully, the body regenerates instead of degenerates, and the body heals. At lower vibrations, the body may experience tension, dis-ease, and chronic pain.

My life changed the day I realized I had a vibration. It went like this. I was visiting a spirituality center that offered a group meditation before their Sunday gathering. I was sitting in a chair in stillness, noticing my breathing and my body, when I suddenly became aware of a vibratory feeling throughout my body. I continued my meditation, and felt my body for the rest of the time. I had this "Aha!" during the meditation, "that I have a vibration!" How cool! I had never felt anything like that before, but I was intrigued. Shortly after that day, I happened to be looking at books online and I came across, *Frequency: The Power of Personal Vibration*, by Penney Pierce. I ordered it and I devoured it. This is representative of how my awakening journey has been. I have an experience, an awareness, or knowing; then shortly after I come across or I am guided to information that confirms my experience.

After my vibration experience, I noticed that every healing, spirituality, and brain health book I came across emphasized the necessity of meditation for realizing or uncovering our true Essence, so I began a meditation practice. When I first started meditating, I would sometimes use guided meditation recordings, but eventually I transitioned to silent meditations. Because I had created so much unhealthy pressure and "shoulds" on myself to "do", having the permission to stop and be still was quite liberating for me. And you have this permission, too! I realized I was forcing life and making it more of a struggle than it needed to be; I welcomed a more relaxed, light, and easy flow. Meditation gave me the space and clarity to make better decisions about where my time is spent, what my priorities are, a deeper sense of the values that are important to me, and most importantly, an inspired and spontaneous approach to living that is energy efficient and purposeful. Not only that, I began to experience emotional and physical healing.

The research on meditation shows numerous health, mental, emotional, and spiritual benefits. From a physical perspective, meditation has been shown to boost the immune system, decrease blood pressure, improve health outcomes in people with chronic dis-ease, reduce obesity, and positively change brain structure and function.

From a mental and emotional perspective, meditation reduces stress, anxiety, depression, and insomnia. Further, meditation boosts positivity, clarity, self-control, emotional intelligence, compassion, insight, and intuition. Spiritually, meditation changes the brain and our energy field so that we can have experiences of God, our spiritual guides, and awaken our healing abilities.

At a certain point in our growth and energetic expansion, we realize that we don't need evidence-based research to decide what we will and won't do. We *know and feel what is best for us*, and we don't have to have blind faith in a God we haven't met - we begin to know and feel our unity with Life Itself, God, the Universe, whatever you want to call it! We operate from an inner knowing, a peaceful and sacred place inside of us that lives us, guides us, and breathes us.

The uncovering of the Godly You is a series of expansions and contractions. There will be times you feel very open, at peace, and alive, and the contractions will feel like, "Oh no, uh, this stuff is up again?" When we are feeling all of the inner and outer drama we've created we can take our consciousness or our awareness out of it, and know that this is not who we truly are or what we have to keep experiencing. The more we realize and practice that the inner and outer drama is an illusion and is not the Truth of the God-self, the more we lessen the energetic power of what we have created, and we can begin creating a life of joy, ease, and wellness.

In addition to meditation and observing the drama of our emotions and our life without giving our power to it, deep breathing is an important pathway to getting out of the body's stress response. When we are stressed or living a limited life, the body is tense, contracted, and we breath shallowly. The more we become aware of our breathing and take more frequent deep breaths, the more we can get out of the stress response and into a rejuvenation and healing mode in the body. Every cell of the body needs oxygen. Being stressed inhibits our cells from getting the oxygen they need. If we pause and take a deep breath when we get triggered and see our trigger as our own trigger to heal, then our strong emotional reactions lose their power and we begin creating a happier, healthier world.

Now, what about fear, worry, anxiety, overwhelm, guilt, shame, angst, and anger?

Ultimately, if it isn't Love, it is fear.

In turning our focus to fully expressing our Godly self, we transcend our fear layer by layer. It is a process, and it can feel like a lot of work at times. But, let's stop making everything such "hard work." If you are committing to living from the Love and bliss of your Godly self, then you really have to choose to feel *everything*. We can't feel the bliss of our Godliness if we won't fully feel the emotions we usually think of as negative, and therefore avoid feeling them. Take an inventory of your habits and see if there are ways you are avoiding fully feeling, and instead, you are numbing yourself. You may become aware that you are using alcohol, drugs, television, exercise, work, busy-ness, and/or perfectionism to keep yourself from feeling the stuff that is uncomfortable. Notice how you feel, what you do, with lightness, in compassion, and without judgment.

I will never forget when I shifted from being "irritated" to truly letting myself feel the anger that was buried inside of me. It was right around my birthday in May, about a year into my spiritual journey. I was driving alone in my car and I had no real reason to feel angry, but it was coming up for me to feel and to heal. The anger I was feeling wasn't about anyone or anything currently going on my life. I had no story to it, and I didn't need to have a story for it. I feel that it is important to own our emotions. I will talk about freeing other people in a later chapter. We have all kinds of triggers and hurt from the past, and if you really let yourself feel, you may be aware that these hurts or strong emotional reactions are not from your current life.

Now I have created a segue into a discussion of past lives. I really would not have believed in past lives if I had not had what I consider a spiritual experience of my past lives.

My family attended a Catholic church in the small town where I was raised. My mom insisted we attend every week while we were growing up, but attendance tapered off as we finished high school. My family didn't talk about our religion at home. I didn't feel really connected to God or have any strong beliefs about what was being taught. In my early twenties, I claimed to be an atheist when any kind of religious conversations came up. I felt that we would die, be buried, and that would be the end of our life. I didn't believe in an afterlife or heaven or hell. However, I began seeking. I would read a book with daily spiritual devotions and affirmations, as well as a book of prayers. I started using a rosary my childhood friend gave to me and I attended a Catholic church in the Twin Cities of Minnesota. I observed people walking out during sermons when the priest spoke negatively about divorce and same-sex relationships. I was looking for true happiness and I noticed that the people didn't seem happy there. I didn't go back.

About a year later I went through a very challenging experience with my graduate school advisor. One night I couldn't sleep, I was crying, and feeling some deep core wounds. I started saying, "God, please help me. Please, please, please. God, please, please help me." Over and over and over. I asked for a sign, saying, "Please give me a sign, please show me. Please help me." After a few moments, I felt a calmness and after a few minutes I felt at ease and ready to sleep. I raised my head to look at the clock, and it read 11:11. As a child, my girlfriends and I always said, "11:11, make a wish!", when we saw that time on the clock. For me, it was my sign from the Universe. I felt like I was heard. I felt more peace than I had felt in a very long time.

The department hired a new faculty member and she wanted me to work with her. Problems persisted with my former advisor, but I was safe, and I ended up with wonderful experiences, grants, travel, and my Doctor of Philosophy in Exercise Physiology with the support of my new advisor. I will come back to this graduate school experience in a later chapter when I talk about freeing others and the forgiveness myth.

So, Life went on. I completed my PhD at age thirty, got married a week later, and we moved to Philadelphia for a postdoctoral research position. My position was all data analysis and manuscript preparation. I didn't need to be on site to do my work, so my mentor let me go back to Minnesota and work remotely part-time. We were back in our house instead of our mouse-infested, studio apartment in Philly. Home Sweet Home!

I gave birth to my first son eleven months after our wedding. Back home from the hospital a couple of days later, I was sitting with him in the rocker, nursing. It was the first time my new baby and I were hanging out alone together. I will never forget this experience. It changed me and opened me up to my Soul. I had this sudden unexpected expansive knowing while looking into my son's eyes that (1) I've known him forever, and (2) I've done this (nursing) before in a past-life. I experienced something bigger than my human self, and I knew that this was not my only life. I knew that I had past lives. I told my mom about this experience and while laughing I said, "I've been reincarnated!" I had heard the term before, but I had no other context around past lives or reincarnation.

Three and a half years later, while I was aware of my spiritual awakening, I read a book about past lives by a psychologist. Then I had some past-life regression sessions when I learned that there was such a thing. The book and the sessions were very healing for me. I also attended a forgiveness workshop that taught that we come into this life with core wounds that we need to heal. We will keep experiencing our core wounds over and over until we heal them. Same stuff, but with different circumstances. We can attract better life experiences and freedom once we have healed our core wounds. Because of my experience with my first son, it was easy for me to see the patterns of my life, take full responsibility for the path of my Soul, and be willing to let go of my hurt.

We will keep experiencing our core wounds over and over until we heal them.

Now here is an important thing about past lives. I feel that we do have some things to go through as a result of what we have done in the past or in past lives. We can clear this karma and change and heal. Some people sense that they have known people for a long time - more of a Soul connection - which I have experienced and feel this is true. However, it is important to not get attached to some sort of story about our past lives or our traumas from of our current life. Let the story go and own the emotions that come up for you. Our emotions and hurt are ours, and it isn't about the current person or experience that is triggering us. If we don't heal our triggers in this circumstance, we are going to keep experiencing our triggers over and over in different scenarios and with different people until we do. It is our same "stuff" showing up with a different face. We are provided with huge opportunities for awesome transformation when we own, feel, and heal our wounds without making it about someone else or blaming them for how we feel.

Our emotions and hurt are ours,
and it isn't about the current person
or experience that is triggering us.

Are you starting to feel into the energetic complexity and multi-dimensional nature of who we are? Can you feel a bit beyond your human-ness? We are energy, we vibrate, and we are Eternal. The physiology of our bodies contributes to how much we can truly know God, and we have some healing to do to fully express our Godliness that was never hurt, does not die, and is and always has been free.

We've created a lot of drama and illusion that doesn't feel that free, and many people aren't living their True self. Our True self, our Godly self, that spark within each and every one of us is Free. The core of your being is free. You are peace. You are balance. You are harmony. You are light. You are abundance. You are grace. You are safe. You are worthy. You are deserving. You are powerful. You are creative. You are brilliant. You are infinite. You are Life Itself.

You are God expressed as You.

In order to be freely authentic and self-actualized, we have to be free from fear, free from hurt, free from blame, and free from hiding. It is time for you to free yourself.

We create our heaven

or we create our hell.

We create our struggle

or we create our ease.

We create our happiness

or we create our pain.

We create our health

or we create our dis-ease.

It is time to take full responsibility for what we are creating. We are powerful creators, co-creating the world, spiraling in perfect energetic alignment. We are magnets, attracting to us what we are. You are the power of Life itself!

Do you want more of the same? Sameness equals safety to your body. The neuropathways of your brain want to do the same things over and over because you wake up alive everyday and doing the same thing has helped you survive. Do you want to survive day by day, recreating your same stuff, or do you want to *thrive blissfully* as the radiantly free Godly You? It is ultimately up to you.

Chapter 3: Free the Mind

Seven years ago I purchased a neat metal wall hanging for our bathroom that had the statement "Live Your Life In The Moment" on it. When I saw it I loved that message and how the colors looked. It added the perfect mix of color to brighten up our tan walls and neutral tile. I liked the concept in this wall hanging, but I was hardly living it! I had no idea that when I bought this wall hanging in 2010, that it would later become representative of how I practice living my daily life, or even that there is specific brain physiology that corresponds to our ability to live happily and freely in the present moment.

I will never forget the day that my life changed as a result of practicing living in the present moment. This is the story of one of my initial spiritual experiences that opened me up to a different reality than I had already been living. I had been reading the book, *The Power of Now: A Guide to Spiritual Enlightenment,* by Eckhart Tolle. It was a life changing book for me, and I read it twice. I think the only other book that I had read twice in my life was To Kill a Mockingbird. I loved that book when I was a kid! I had read *The Power of Now* on my own, and then my book club was reading it. I wanted to read it again and I got even more out of it. I hope you read this book twice! Hehe!

One afternoon, I was home with my two boys, who were one and three years of age at the time, and I realized that I wasn't being very present with them. I was a good mom doing the mom thing, but I always let myself have something on my mind. They were playing on the living room floor and I was finding things to do. I thought, okay, I am going to try this "being present" thing out. I didn't have anything that I "had" to do, so intentionally I brought my awareness to the present moment. I simply observed the boys for a few moments. I was standing by the kitchen counter, trying out the present moment thing, and I suddenly felt this weight lift off of me. It was the energy of letting things "weigh on me." I felt instantly lighter and I stood up straighter and felt taller. I found that I could breathe better also.

The Power of Now didn't tell me that would happen. But I had read enough about our energy field that I knew that energetically, I had become lighter and clearer. I felt that I had experienced an instantaneous healing. So much of our attention is on the past or the future. We can't do anything about what has happened in the past, but we humans give so much power away when we continue to ruminate, let ourselves get emotionally triggered, or start thinking about our regrets and should haves. We also have a tendency to invest so much of our energy into what hasn't happened yet. This creates overwhelm and worry that takes away from our ability to feel the joy and freedom of living in the present moment.

Through my meditation practice and in getting Higher Brain Living® sessions, I have gained much more awareness as to where I am putting my attention and what I am doing with my mind. I notice very quickly where my mind is and I have a moment-to-moment practice of living in the present moment throughout the day. I used to not be able to focus in depth on anything if my children were around. If I wanted to read something that took concentration, such as a research article, or if I was trying to do some writing, I wasn't able to focus until my children were in bed. Living in the present moment has enabled me to live more spontaneously and inspired. I will sometimes write down tasks if I want to make sure to respond to an email or to call someone back. However, my life isn't driven by my to-do lists or over planning my days. I am able to go with the flow and get things done, handling whatever things are "meant to be" taken care of in each moment. I'm not saying throw out the planner! I'm just saying to trust the flow and what you need to know will come to you as you go. Just feel for what is the best next step.

Living in the present moment enables us to live more spontaneously and inspired.

Super Brain, by Deepak Chopra, a spiritual teacher, and Dr. Rudolph Tanzi, a Harvard brain researcher, talks about how multi-tasking is very much a habit of the lower brain. When we are operating from higher-brain functioning, our attention is present on one task at a time. Surprisingly, they also describe to-do lists and grocery lists as having a negative effect on the brain. Ideally, it is good for the brain to think and recall spontaneously and in the moment. I noticed that how I do my calendar has changed. I used to always have a paper and pencil calendar book that I would carry in my purse. I could see an entire week at a time. In graduate school, with assignments and the research studies I was coordinating, I would look at my calendar and feel overwhelmed. I would stress and be heavy over a presentation that I had to give that was a month away. Now, I use the calendar on my iPhone and I generally look at one day at a time. For me, this way of seeing one day at a time has helped me to be present to one day at a time instead of focusing on weeks and months. And I don't procrastinate like I used to either. I feel that eliminating the sense of overwhelm has helped me to perceive tasks as less daunting. Over time, practicing living in the present moment becomes easier and easier, and it makes life lighter and freer. Overwhelm, worry, stress, control, and anxiety lose their power over us.

How we perceive our life, our circumstances, our children, our boss, etc. is largely determined by how we have been "wired", that is we've created our neuropathways to keep doing the same thing over and over and experiencing life the same way, because that has kept us alive - remember sameness = safety. But we can choose to start responding a new way and choose to create more lightheartedness and ease in our lives. First, we need to know that we can create a life that is easy; we don't have to create struggle or a "hard life." Wouldn't it feel better to flow in life with ease rather than with struggle? Further, it is our perception that changes, not necessarily the circumstances. However, as we begin seeing our life as beautiful, then the problems just magically begin to fix themselves. And, when we align our energy at a very high frequency vibration, flow, ease, and peace happen organically.

We need to know that we can create a life that is easy; we don't have to create struggle or a hard life.

Now, one of the shifts of perception that must happen in order to spiritually expand is to realize that we are not victims of life, other people, our bodies, a condemning God, or that we were dealt a bad hand. That is not true and those beliefs are very disempowering to ourselves. Consider that our Souls are on a journey and have lessons to learn. I have felt that on the soul level we choose our parents and some of our major life experiences in order to experience and heal our Soul's core wounds. We may keep experiencing these same wounds in different circumstances and with different people until we shift our perception and heal the energies in us that are attracting circumstances that reflect what is going on within us. We are energetic magnets attracting that which we are. Our energy field holds all of our energetic imprints that attract to us our circumstances in energetic perfection and beauty. You may have heard or read of the The Law of Attraction in another place. Energetically and spiritually, the Law of Attraction runs deep, and we are powerful attractors through our beliefs, words, and thoughts, much of which we have allowed to run the show unconsciously.

You may be familiar with the teaching of Jesus, "It is done unto you as you believe." Henry Ford said, "Whether you think you can or you can't, you're right." Since we were born, we've created conditioning and stories about ourselves and life. Much of what we are operating from is subconscious, meaning many of us humans don't even know *why we do what we do*. Life is a perfect reflection of us. Therefore, our mind is powerful, and we create a life in response to what we are putting out.

I remember having moments of feeling completely overwhelmed with the responsibility of being responsible for what I experience. It didn't last long, because we go on living day by day. Although, once we know this, there is no option but to take every thought, word, and belief we notice ourselves expressing and question whether this is what we really want to create for ourselves. I will say that there were times when I have felt that observing and clearing out my mental clutter was the single most challenging thing I have ever done. And then, I had to decide to stop telling myself mind mastery is challenging! We are also inundated by social constructs and we have to decide if we want all of that to be true for us, or not.

When we get extremely clear and conscious of how we are using our thoughts and words, we get into the space of self-mastery, and we can begin putting out there exactly what it is we want to create. *This is the shift from victim to creator.*

Now that we know our beliefs, thoughts, and words are powerful, we can begin to create a new expression for ourselves. One tool that I have used quite a bit is affirmations. You may have read about affirmations, tried them out, or written some down. But now is the time to start creating anew. I am going to dive into this, but I am not going to call them affirmations. They are about affirming what we sincerely wish to create, however let's now really utilize the power of our mind. Using affirmative statements as a starting point to a deeper dig into ourself is powerful. As we use them, we can begin to notice the places in our lives where things are not showing up in a positive way. The mind is powerful and we co-create our experience with Life Itself, so now I will introduce the tool I call "Recreators" to shift what we have already created into intentionally creating our radiance, our health, our joy, and our peace.

In order to put the Recreators into use, we have to decide to use them and override our usual mental chatter. Also, every time we become aware of something in our life that isn't showing up in the direction that we desire, we must implement the use of a Recreator to tell our energy and our body and new story.

Check out my app for Apple and Android, and subscribe to get daily Recreators, Power Words, and growth messages from me to assist you in creating your Godly potential. For the details, visit www.rachelapp.com.

A number of years ago, I took a class called, The Foundations of Science of Mind. The premise of the class was that we put our thoughts (seeds), into the neutral subjective law (soil), and produce our experience (plant). Each of us did a final project for the class and one woman made bookmarks and gave one to everyone in the class. The bookmarks had a yellow ribbon and the phrase, Life Is So Easy For Me, was typed on them. I loved it. To this day, I often use this statement.

Even though I didn't have a lot of very bad things happen to me during my life, I still perceived life as being quite a struggle. Pain is pain, hurt is hurt, and overwhelm is overwhelm, regardless of the circumstance. There was a period during my early days as a mother, when my kids were very little and before I had become aware of my awakening, that I was just trying to get through the day. I wanted to survive the day so that I could get them into bed so I could chill out, rest up, and get ready to try to survive the next day. *I was perceiving my day-to-day life as a struggle*.

**We don't just have to survive
and get through the day.
We can thrive, feel fulfilled, and live happily
even in the midst of change and challenge.**

If there are areas of your life that you perceive as a struggle or if you are aware that you have a perception that life is hard or life is a struggle, you can now start using the recreator, *Life is so easy for me.* Take some deep breaths and say, *Life is so easy for me*, over and over until you feel more relaxed. I used a version of this recreator earlier today. I went away to spend some quiet time writing this book, but I was feeling the old heaviness that I had around writing to accomplish something. I started saying to myself, *Writing books and being an author is so easy for me*.

I will give examples of recreators as they pertain to various areas throughout the rest of this book. While we are here in the chapter, Free the Mind, I want to let you know that you are brilliant, creative, and capable. Every single one of us is. We all have our own unique gifts and place in the world. There is ultimately no competition, we are simply creating our own experience and we all have our own unique path.

- Have you believed that you are not smart or as smart as someone else?
- Have you believed that there is something that you want to do but you think you can't?

- Is there something that you would like to do but you have believed that it would be too hard or that it would be too much to do?

Through my experience, I have come to know that we all have our own inner-genius. Yes, every single one of us. If it is in you or I, then it is in everyone else, and no one is better than anyone else. We all just have a different purpose and have chosen to play a certain role. If you are finding that you are not expressing your inner-genius, then you likely have beliefs about yourself that are blocking you from fully expressing your Godly potential and the wisdom that goes with it. We don't necessarily need more education or training to express our Godly potential, but we have to stop believing that we can't or that others have something that we don't. Most importantly, don't let something someone may have said in the past determine what you think you are capable of. The more we get out of our lower brain habits and untruths, the more we unwind and release the energies blocking and keeping us from our Godly creativity, our intuition, our insight, and our brilliance.

Every single one of us

has our own inner-genius.

Try some of these recreators when you find yourself blocking the flow of your inner-genius:

I am intuitive and wise.

I easily express my inner-genius.

I am brilliantly bringing my gifts to the world.

I am peaceful and present.

I am calm and knowing.

I trust and I let go.

I am brilliantly creative in my own unique way.

My genius is sourced through God.

The answers come to me at the perfect time.

I can do anything that I am called to do.

I am fully capable of a thriving life.

It is safe for me to be me.

I am heard, honored, and respected.

I see the brilliance in everyone.

All is well.

Chapter 4: Free the Body

We can truly trust our body; it is an amazing and beautiful machine that enables us to live, move, and be Love in the world.

Our bodies are innately wise and our bodies speak to us. It is quite common in our society, and especially in the health and fitness industry, that we ignore what our body is saying to us. We may have created a tendency to either completely dominate our body or numb ourselves out. We haven't been taught to trust our bodies and so it is common that we don't pay attention to the signals from our body. We can truly trust our body; it is an amazing and beautiful machine that enables us to live, move, and be in the world.

Let yourself take a moment and feel a bit of awe at how the body innately knows how to

grow and how to heal. Let yourself be grateful for this gift, your amazing body, that has carried you up to this point in your life. Thank your body today and every day.

True beauty comes from the inside - and honoring, accepting, and appreciating our body makes us more radiant and improves the body's ability to heal. Our bodies know what they need, so we can let it tell us when it needs movement and when it needs rest. Our bodies tell us when we are hungry or thirsty, or when we are satisfied. It will also tell us what to eat, and this won't be as rigid and restrictive as the nutrition field has led us to believe. Further, our bodies are very unique, so one-size-fits-all approaches might work for a while, but they won't be lasting. Only YOU can truly feel and know what your body is telling you.

I have always found the human body fascinating. In high school, I loved biology and ended up attending a university my senior year to take

Biology 101. I continued in college with human anatomy and physiology classes. Life led me into getting a Doctor of Philosophy degree (PhD) in Exercise Physiology. I started teaching group fitness classes at a gym when I was 17 years old. I knew all the rules, *shoulds,* and recommendations when it came to the human body.

Over the years my weight went up, and down, and up, and down, and up and down by about 15 pounds. I have been generally healthy, but experienced colds and coughing at the end of every school semester. I had mononucleosis (mono) in high school, as an undergraduate, and again after I had my first son and was working on my postdoctoral research. "They" say you can only have mono once, but I was diagnosed with it three times. I was living a life of burnout and forcing myself to do what I thought I "should" do, instead of trusting and honoring my own body.

We are unlimited in energy as long as we are not blocked, not giving our power away, and not living out of alignment with our Godliness.

It was very liberating for me to learn about energy healing and that we can heal energetic blockages in our energy field. We are unlimited in energy as long as we are not blocked, not giving our power away, and not living out of alignment with our Godliness. Doing too much and spreading ourselves too thin drains us. If you can't trust your body yet, trust me and start trusting that Life, God, the Universe, whatever you want to call IT, will guide you and support you in healing your body and your energy field, as well as shaping your life into an experience of lightness, joy, purpose, fulfillment, and ease.

The health and radiance of our bodies is not solely determined by diet and exercise. There are emotional, energetic, and mental aspects to tune into as well. In the last chapter, I wrote about the power of our beliefs, thoughts, and words for creating our lives. *The power of our beliefs, thoughts, and words applies to our bodies as well.*

Our bodies want to be harmonious, balanced, healthy, and radiant, and our bodies can be that way if we are honoring, loving, and being truthful to the body. The Truth is that you are all that God is and the essence of who you really are is radiantly well and radiantly beautiful. There has never been and never will be anything wrong with you. That inner-spark in you, your God self, was and is never hurt - was and is never ill - was and is never anything but Love. We have mistakenly misaligned ourselves with the fear, drama, and dis-ease, instead of aligning with the radiant Essence of who we really are.

Let's create our radiant health from the Truth of who we are.

All that is, Is God. That is, everything in the known universe is made up of God stuff, or the energy of Life Itself. And this also includes our food. In order to feel and know what our own body really wants, we have to let go of our definitions of food as good or bad, healthy or unhealthy, and clean or dirty. We have to make the shift from fear of food to love, enjoyment, and gratitude for our food. We have to stop defining our day by whether we think we made "good" choices with food so we had a "good" day, or we think we made "bad" choices with food so we had a "bad" day.

I don't have a scale in my home. It isn't good for our bodies to feel bad about who much we weigh. We can't unconditionally accept ourselves if we are defining our self-worth by a number on a scale. Consider getting rid of your scale so that you stop judging yourself as "good" because you are at the weight you want to be at, or "bad" because you are not at the weight you want to be.

You can stop fearing food, because food in and of itself does not make us fat. And also, be aware of what you are believing as you are eating. If you eat candy, are you believing that you are bad, that it will make you fat, and/or the sugar will kill you? That is not what you want to create for your body, so be grateful for the beautiful sugar treats God has given us. When we stop making ourselves wrong for what we are eating or how we think we look, we can heal our shame.

When we believe that "I am bad," we are giving our power to shame. And, when we are focused on believing that "I am bad, because I ate sugar," we are giving our power to guilt. When we are in these beliefs around ourselves and food, then we create what I call *Shame Cycling*. Giving our power to shame makes us keep doing exactly what it is that we don't want to be doing. When we eat something in love and gratitude we can have it, enjoy it, and let it satisfy us. When we eat something in shame, guilt, or fear, we tend to keep doing exactly what we are shaming ourselves for - hence, the Shame Cycle.

For example, let's say there is a pan of brownies on the counter. A balanced and harmonious approach to brownies on the counter would be to notice the brownies, go within yourself and ask whether that even sounds or feels good at this moment. If "yes," then take a brownie, walk away from the pan of brownies, sit at the table, taste how delicious it is, be present and in the moment while enjoying the brownie, thank God for the beautiful food such as brownies that we can eat, notice when the brownie has satisfied our bellies and satiated our taste buds, then stop eating when the brownie no longer tastes good or our belly feels content.

Now consider the following approach. A disharmonious approach to brownies on the counter would be noticing the brownies, impulsively rushing over to the brownies, thinking I should not eat this brownie, taking a brownie and eating it while standing by the brownie pan, thinking about work or the kids or the past, thinking I'm so bad for eating this, taking another brownie, eating it while standing by the brownie pan, thinking about the big project you have to work on that is yet a month away, finishing the brownie, and start thinking how bad you are because you ate two brownies - and you want to eat another one and thinking that would be so bad and I shouldn't.

Do you feel the difference in these two approaches to food? This applies to anything we are eating. First, we have to stop judging food as good or bad, it is all energy and it is all Go(o)d. Second, we have to be present in the moment with our beautiful food, and enjoy the taste and be grateful. Approach food in love, gratitude, and trust. Deepak Chopra has said that it is the *fear of food* that is more harmful to us than the food itself.

I had a spiritual experience around food at a school fundraiser at my son's school. The Dads group was raising money for the family of a student who was ill. It took place in the spring, in the back of the school by the playground. They were serving hot dogs, chips, candy, and orange drink from McDonalds. It was every health nuts greatest nightmare. While my boys and I were sitting on the ground, enjoying our hot dogs, I had an experience of the God in everything. There are not words for experiences like this, but I will try to put words to it and say that I felt the lightness, connection, and Grace in all the food and in all the people that were there. I also had a chuckle while eating the hot dog when I thought about all the people who *wouldn't dare* eat a hot dog.

Eating a hot dog (or some other food that you have defined as unhealthy) here and there is not going to harm you. However, if hot dogs (or some other food) are the only thing you really want to eat, then maybe consider becoming aware of an emotional or spiritual component. Take note of what you have determined to be healthy. Which is healthier - broccoli or a hamburger? Most people would reply the broccoli is healthier than a hamburger. However, what if there are times when the body needs broccoli so broccoli would be in your body's greatest good? And, what if there are times when your body may need the protein, iron, and grounding of a hamburger (such as around your menstrual cycle if you are a woman), so then a hamburger would be in your body's greatest good? This concept doesn't support restrictive and rigid eating habits, or eating plans that don't allow you to enjoy the foods you love. If there is something your body needs, trust that Life will guide you to it.

A while ago when I shared a blog I wrote about past-lives, a friend of mine shared with me that after she read my blog, she had an awareness that what she called "a sugar addiction" was from a past life. It was so cool to hear that she was able to have this awareness about herself after reading about past-lives in my blog. I don't feel that food or sugar is innately addictive. We humans are addictive, and there is something deeper going on emotionally or spiritually if we are overly attracted to something.

If we are truly present with our bodies and the food that we are eating in any given moment, we will notice that at some point the food loses its appeal. That is because our taste buds become de-sensitized when our body no longer needs more of a certain food. We will notice that the food no longer provides the same beautiful taste, so we don't need more of it. And, we may notice that our belly feels satisfied, so we don't need to finish everything that is on our plate if it no longer sounds good or gives us a good internal feeling.

Trust that food is good and necessary. It is nourishing and provides energy for us to live. The metabolism of the body is like a fire; it needs fuel to keep burning. The more we workout and live an active lifestyle, the more food (a.k.a. fuel) we will need. If we are not very active the less fuel we will need. The body knows how much fuel we need. It tells us to fuel up when we are hungry and it tells us when we are satisfied. Avoid counting and cutting calories; tune into the cues from your own body instead. Question all-or-nothing ideas, such as the fat-free movement of the 1990's, the carb-free movement of the 2000's, and the detox, gluten-free, and dairy-free movement of the 2010's. The body needs calories in the form of protein, fat, and carbohydrates for fuel. I suggest that we put our attention more on loving ourself, being grateful for whatever food is available to us, and embrace lighthearted and easy living. That is where healing happens.

A couple of years ago, I had a conversation with a woman at a conference. We were talking about what we do, and when I told her that I am passionate about helping people follow their own intuition to what their body needs, she shared her experience. She told me that she had a sensitivity to gluten, but that it went away when she healed her grief over her father's death. I share this to highlight that if there is a food that our body is resisting, it may be that there is something emotional or spiritual that is causing it. Because, in a healed happy state, our bodies can process life and all food in a joyous, healthy way, and we have awesome organs and systems that are designed to do that for us. It is also very important to believe that food is not innately harmful. The more we heal and clear our energy field, we may organically be attracted to new foods and habits that honor the body, but it is not necessary to completely restrict what we use as fuel for our body.

Now let's move onto movement. At high levels of consciousness - that is, joy, love, bliss, gratitude, and compassion - the body experiences joyful movement free from pain and dis-ease. When we shift our fears to Love, healing happens. This is what we would call a miracle. I believe that any healing is possible. It is important that we notice where we are numbing ourselves and/or dominating our bodies. Our health and fitness industry teaches us to do more and more and more with our bodies, yet that may not really be serving ourselves, our families, and the True needs of our body. If we are obsessed with any activity on the extreme end, such as marathon running, we may need to look at what we are trying to escape or what we are running away from. Our bodies don't require that much physical activity for healthy, balanced living. In contrast, if we aren't inspired to move our bodies at all, we may have a belief that we are not good enough to do some activity. We are fully capable of walking out in nature, dancing in the privacy of our own home, and expressing joyful movement in the body.

When I began listening to my body and started following my intuition, I retired from teaching group fitness classes after 18 years. I learned that my body did not need to workout that intensely and for that long. When I later attended a group fitness class at a gym, I observed the instructor yelling at the class, the loud music, and the other participants in the class. Being out of dominating instructor mode allowed me to witness the insanity of the group exercise setting. We numb ourselves out and distract ourselves with the loud music, we think that harder and more intense is better, and we keep going when our bodies have had enough. At forty-five minutes, I could see that the class participants' bodies were done and had enough. But, the class continued and the instructor even went ten minutes over the sixty minutes end time.

In the past I always wanted an hour workout, it had to be intense, with music in my ears, and I valued running over walking. My body had tension and tightness in my muscles and I was very inflexible. Now I have slowed down, backed off on the intensity, and I tune into my body. After allowing my body to rest and rejuvenate for a couple of years, and healing from the inside out, I am much happier, more flexible, and more creative and open with my movement. I have started doing freestyle movement (dancing), going for walks, gentle yoga, and some strength exercises. Moreover, as a mom, I noticed that I had more energy throughout the day instead of having my body conserve the energy for the intense exercise sessions that I used to force myself to do.

When I got out of the rigid choreographed movements from my group exercise training, my body started wanting dance on its own. I have followed my body's lead on this, because I would not have started doing this on my own. In my twenties I enjoyed a bit of alcohol, and I definitely needed to be drinking to lose my inhibitions on the dance floor. I have noticed that we keep our body in rigid patterns of movement because that is safe. What if we didn't need alcohol to free our inhibitions and move joyfully? What if we weren't afraid of what we think people might think? What if we weren't afraid to be playful and be free? If you are one of those people who are unwilling to dance at all or unwilling to dance without alcohol, my suggestion would be to go a bit deeper into yourself and realize that there is a part of you that either believes you can't dance or believes you are not safe and you are afraid of what other people think. You can liberate yourself from these limitations. It is simply a choice and it is up to you. Dance it out!

A lot of time and energy is currently being invested into our bodies. People are running marathons, competing in body appearance competitions, and spending hours per day at the gym or doing physical activity. I think it is important to ask ourselves if this aligns with the Highest Good for the use of our time and energy. As I mentioned earlier, when I cut back on the frequency and intensity of my physical movement, I found myself with much more energy throughout the entire day.

Mothering small children is very physically demanding and at the time I probably didn't need to then chase to the gym in the evening. I had more energy for living, being with and enjoying my kids, for household tasks, for learning new things, and for writing this book!

An unlimited Source of energy is wanting to pour through us for our Highest, most purposeful living. If we are not expressing that, then we are wasting energy somewhere and/or giving our power away. Furthermore, if we have some sort of definition that we should be living like the Energizer Bunny and hyper-enthusiastic all the time, then we may want to redefine what powerfully energetic, healthy, and content living looks like. Our bodies need rest, too. Our bodies need calm. Our bodies need us to be present and aware of them. Go, go, go is not in the best interests of the wellness of the body. Health and harmony happens from a balance of rest and joyful movement.

If you are finding that you are having trouble getting moving and/or you are making excuses to even go for a walk, then your beliefs and emotions may be getting in your way. See if you may be operating from an all-or-nothing approach, perfectionism, or shame. Are you numbing out in front of the television when your body would really love to dance? Shame and perfectionism prevents us from wanting to take action. Know that you don't have to run marathons to be healthy and lean. Be willing to try something new. Our bodies want to move and express in all kinds of diverse ways. They don't want to do the same thing or the same movement pattern over and over and over. There may be a growth opportunity in moving in more than one way or in learning a new movement pattern.

It takes a lot of energy to grow big muscles and lift a lot of weight. Perhaps the images in the magazines aren't what our bodies are truly biologically designed to do. For instance, I personally don't find the overly huge muscles on men to be attractive. Is this excessive muscle necessary for daily living? The answer is no. So why are we investing so much energy at the gym. Is there a place in our lives where our energy and effort might contribute more to our Highest good and the good of the world around us? Further, might we be forcing our bodies into lower-brain fight or flight, by doing too much fight movements, such as kickboxing, or too much flight, such as running?

There is a harmonious balance that our bodies already know and will speak to us if we pay attention.

Meditation is an excellent way to start *tuning in* instead of trying to keep up with the beliefs, constructs, shoulds, and rules we have created for ourselves.

- Our bodies know if we do or don't need a medication.

- Our bodies know if we do or don't need a medical procedure.
- Our bodies know if we need a hamburger or some broccoli.
- Our bodies know if we need to run or walk.
- Our bodies know when it is time to sleep or when it is time to do.

None of these are good or bad options, but our radiant wellness is in aligning with what would be most honoring to each of our own bodies. Let's love and trust our amazing bodies.

Here are some recreators you can use for recreating your health and your body:

My body is radiantly well.

My body is harmonious, balanced, and alive.

My body is easily expressing my ideal body weight.

My body is healthy and well in every single cell.

All the food I eat is used and eliminated in perfect digestion.

My body is flexible, lean, and beautiful.

Life lives through me and I am free.

All of the organs in my body are operating at optimal function.

My body is youthful and living happily.

I am energetically clear and I radiate Love.

I know what is for the Highest Good of my body.

I easily act on what my body requests.

I am healed.

I trust life and I trust my body.

I am forever well.

Chapter 5: Free You

*Creating a happy life you love
starts with you and only you.*

Self-liberation. You are the only one who can free
yourself. Each of us has to make the choice to
start creating lightness, peace, and freedom in our
lives. It is up to us, and it doesn't have to do with
anyone else - not our spouse, not our parents, not
our friends, not our boss, not our children, and not
the traffic. Creating a happy life you love starts
with you and only you. It is an inside job, because
what is going on within us creates a life that is
reflective of us on the outside.

We have the potential to live from Love - the
unconditional, defenseless, and unattached kind of
Love. This state has been called enlightenment.
This is the ultimate goal of personal and spiritual
development, as well as the human potential

movement. If indeed we get going on developing ourselves, at a certain point, when enough shifts have been made, the journey turns into a spiritual one. We have the potential to move from our greatest human potential, to what I call our Godly potential. One of the greatest shifts and gifts you can bring to your life is to choose self-love and self-acceptance. We can't fully and freely love others until we have chosen to fully and freely accept ourselves. You can know this, but putting it into practice certainly changes things.

Let's choose self-acceptance. It is such a powerful thing to do. Being grateful for who we are, and for this body to live in, heals us and empowers us.

When we truly accept ourselves, we don't have to wear any masks or try to be anything but ourselves.

One of the masks that some humans wear is the mask of confidence. An authentic, loving, and empowered confidence comes when we love and accept ourselves, but there is a confidence mask as well. This mask looks like trying so hard, intense, an over do-er, trying to prove, and a fast-talker. When you are with a person with this kind of mask, you may be wanting to say, "Hey, would it be okay for us to just stop and pause for a moment. Can we stop and take a deep breath?" This mask is a forced confidence, when really on the inside the person is not feeling good about themselves. Liberating ourselves from this mask, opens us up to vulnerability, authenticity, and freedom. Additionally when we let go of needing to fake it, our energy can be used in a more efficient way in our self-expression. For a time, a day, or a week, we may feel really raw and exposed. And that is okay. Just allow and let yourself be okay with just *being present as you,* without having to prove yourself, accomplish anything, or try to be perceived a certain way that you have defined as "good."

Authentic and liberated confidence comes when we surrender our small-selves to our greater self, that is, our God-self. Energetically, this is a huge shift. It requires a lot of energy to keep a mask in place. We wear masks anytime we are doing or being in a way that is not in alignment with what is true for us. On the other hand, if we are living life not feeling very confident and comfortable in our own skin, we may be choosing to stay comfortable, not taking risks, and playing it safe. We make huge forward leaps in our lives when we are willing to say "yes" to things that make us uncomfortable.

Our greatest growth happens
when we are willing to
step into whatever scares us the most.

I was terribly shy in high school, but when a gym owner asked me if I would train to teach group fitness classes, I said "yes." For the first few months, I had diarrhea before every class that I taught. I was scared, yet I grew. I continued to say yes and more opportunities came my way because of it. Our greatest growth happens when we are willing to step into whatever scares us the most. I have learned to get really comfortable with being uncomfortable. I know that the biggest difference between someone who finishes what they set out to do, and those who don't is the belief that they "can." With time and practice, we can rewire our brains to do what we are guided to do.

I would see this "I can" mentality show up when I was teaching Zumba group fitness classes. When I first started going to Zumba classes, I didn't know the moves. I couldn't keep up. However, I liked the music and I thought the teacher was awesome, so I kept going back each week. After a couple of months, I learned her moves and was able to keep up. After a few months, I looked like I knew what I was doing. Eventually, I became trained in Zumba and I started teaching classes. I was shocked at how many people would come to one Zumba class and decide that they couldn't do it and would not come back again. We don't have to work so hard at things. This isn't about mastery or being perfect. Simply trying - and a bit of consistency - will result in you learning something new and giving you forward growth. This isn't just about Zumba, this is about the inner belief that *you can*. And, you can! I know you can!

Tell yourself that you can do whatever is yours to do.

One of the greatest shifts in freeing ourselves comes when we choose to stop feeling bad about ourselves. Yes, this is a choice - a simple choice. About a month after I had my second son, I noticed that I was feeling icky about how my body looked. I made the choice then and there that I was going to stop having negative feelings about my body. I was thirty-three at the time and I thought, "I don't want to continue into the next part of my life continuing this cycle of feeling bad about how I look." My weight had fluctuated up and down over the years, and now after having another baby I didn't want to give so much energy to an over-focus on my body. I remember thinking, "Gosh, here I have two beautiful babes that love me and a husband who loves me regardless of what my body is doing, I am going to freakin' love and be okay with me, too."

We have to have a bit of self awareness to observe how we are operating, see that it isn't serving us, and then choose a new way of being. It may take a bit of practice, but as time goes on we start to eliminate the negativity toward ourselves and we free up a lot of wasted energy. As we commit to self-love, we will start to see all of the places we aren't being in Love.

As we take notice of how we are feeling, we can breathe and know this isn't the Truth of who we are, we gradually heal over time.

A good check point in determining how we are doing with self-love is taking notice of how critical we are of others. When we are critical of others, we are projecting our self-hatred out there. This criticism of others is a reflection of our own self-criticism. We don't want to feel how icky we feel on the inside, so the human response is to focus on what we don't like in others. If you are finding yourself overly critical of others, see if you can try to see the Go(o)d in them instead. I love how "Namaste" is used in yoga classes - I bow to you and honor the light and love in you that is the same as the light and love in me. At the level of our Godly self, we are all made of exactly the same stuff. What we don't like in others is somewhere in our self. When we are able to start seeing the stuff in ourselves that we don't like in others, we start getting really, really, humble, much more accepting of others, and much more accepting and loving to ourselves. *Focus on you, not them.*

Do you compare yourself to others? If yes, then please stop. You dishonor and disempower yourself when you compare yourself to others. You have no need to compare and contrast yourself to other people. Everyone is uniquely beautiful, and that also includes you. We all have our innate genius and brilliance, and that includes you, too. We all are a unique expression of God, and that includes you, too. Over 500 million sperm were racing to the egg in your mother and you won the race. Why you? You are here for a reason, and to give the unique gifts that only you can give. There are no accidents and nothing happens by random chance.

Be grateful that you are even here at all, because you are a miracle.

When we choose self-love, we are making the conscious choice to make a huge shift in our consciousness. We will be less and less likely to get stuck in lower levels of consciousness, such as fear, doubt, guilt, and shame. We end up having a solid foundation that allows us to take bold steps in our life.

- As our vibration shifts when we are at higher levels of consciousness, what we attract into our life changes.
- As we heal those parts of us that have been wounded, life gets easier because we are no longer attracting circumstances that reflect our wounds.

The more we accept ourselves, that more we will come to know that we are lovable and we are worthy. If we are truly committed to our path of becoming radiantly free, then we are going to have to feel all the aspects of ourselves that we have kept hidden. This concept has been called *the shadow* by other authors and philosophers.

As I have experienced expanded states of gratitude, unconditional Love, and connection, the more I am able to dig deeper and feel the parts of myself that are uncomfortable. Once we expand and vibrate at a higher level, we shake loose the dense lower energy aspects that need to be cracked open and liberated. Ultimately, we want to purge everything out of our energy field and our mind that is not Pure Love.

Worthiness is one of the core wounds of humanity. I attended a demonstration of a healing technique where I learned more about my own constructs of being worthy. The woman leading the education session asked me to serve as her demonstrator for the technique. I was delighted! But more importantly, I was open and ready to shift whatever was going to come up for me.

She was using the technique of muscle testing (a.k.a. applied kinesiology), to determine what trapped emotions, beliefs, and blocks could be healed during the session. I held my arm out to the side, and if my arm stayed strong when she pushed down on it then that indicated *yes*. If my arm would go weak and drop when she said a statement, it indicated *no*, and she would perform an energetic clearing and shifting.

She began the process, teaching and explaining as she went. She came to the question of worthiness, and she said "I am worthy." My arm stayed strong and I felt on the inside that, "yes I am worthy." Next, she said, "I am worthy of the kingdom of God." This time my arm dropped, and I found myself bursting into tears. I was able to feel that I did not believe on a subconscious level that I was worthy of the kingdom of God. She facilitated an energy healing to clear that for me. So cool! Of note, this technique can also be used to tap into the wisdom of the body and test whether there are any supplements or medications our body may need, or we can test if anything else is right for us or not. I use it on my own to test whether my decisions are in my Highest Good. It has helped me to trust my decisions and let go of worry and doubt.

Over time, through meditation, self-awareness, prayer, and other techniques we can become more and more conscious of the beliefs and programming that don't align with our greatest good.

A complete and utter freedom can live and move through us if we let it. Know that there is nothing wrong with you. We are ultimately safe and ultimately free. Our soul doesn't die, so we don't even need to fear death. This life we are living is like a movie playing on a screen that we perceive as reality. It is an illusion. However, the greater spiritual Reality is that we are the watcher of the movie, and that watcher is the peace, Love, and light that we came from. And, we will return to our true home when our soul chooses. Inner freedom is alive for us when we shift from fear to Love.

The following recreators can assist you in freeing yourself:

I am Love.

I accept myself as I am.

I am accepting and loving to all.

I am worthy.

I am happy and free in my body.

I radiate love wherever I go.

I love being me.

I fully live my Godly nature.

I am grateful and glad to be me.

I take bold steps in the direction of my dreams.

My path is crystal clear.

I live lightheartedly.

I can be, do, and have anything.

I am radiantly free.

I can do whatever I am called to do.

Chapter 6: Free Others

When we are able to discontinue allowing other people to have power over our emotions and reactions, we free them and we free ourselves. This is a powerful healing. You might be surprised to hear this from a Reverend, but I will go ahead here and say, "*forgiveness is a myth.*" I attended a forgiveness workshop that changed my life and *shifted my perception from victim to creator.* Yet ultimately we come to the realization that there is nothing to forgive. You can call some of our experiences with other people soul contracts, karmic agreements, and/or law of attraction. But whatever the energetic connection between others and us, it happens in perfect alignment, and it has been perfectly co-created between both souls.

We free others by taking full responsibility for our role in the connection and whatever our souls need to play out for our evolution.

I am going to share a bit of my own life experience for the purpose of illustrating how I was able to heal by shifting my perception. I had a heck of an experience with a graduate school advisor. Our working relationship started out great, but it took a turn for the worse. I mentioned this in an earlier chapter when I shared my 11:11 experience in graduate school. Just for context, while I was in graduate school, I had an assistantship, so I was working, teaching, and had an office space on campus. Everything that went on doesn't matter at this point in my growth, although I will share that even after I had a new advisor, the first advisor was still in the same laboratory area. One day an undergraduate student was doing some work on a study that I was overseeing. He was using my officemate's computer.

This professor came into my office space very upset and said that the undergraduate student is not allowed to work on my officemate's computer.

He didn't let me say anything, and every time I tried he would get more and more defensive and angry. It was so uncomfortable that I stood up to leave the office, but I heard a voice from within speak to me and say, "Stop, this is your office space." So I stopped, and in that moment this professor proceeded to yell in my face while pointing his finger two inches from my face, "You sit down! You sit down! You sit down!" It was crazy - and he didn't stop. I stood in my power and calmly interjected with my voice shaking, "You can't tell me to sit down." He continued, "You sit down…!" and I interjected, saying, "You can't tell me to sit down." I had never experienced something like this before and I certainly would not have expected it in a university setting.

I wasn't the only person who had an issue with this professor. Four other graduate students had changed advisors also, and other professors and department staff were also having negative experiences with him. After that incident, he was moved out of the lab space and into another building. The office of Equal Employment Opportunity wanted me to go forward with an investigation. I didn't. While there were several witnesses to this incident and other things, it would have been my word against his. I didn't feel that this had to be all on me, since I wasn't the only person who had experienced issues with him. He had been moved out of the lab, so I felt safe. I let it go.

But, I realized that I didn't let it go. I had been traumatized. Is this stuff actually allowed in the workplace? Nothing prepares us for something like this. I had held back and I didn't speak up sooner. So, life made me speak up. Unfortunately, it took this kind of circumstance for me to do so.

I completed my degree with my new fabulous advisor. The years went on. I continued ruminating about this experience, and I was giving my power away to it. One day, in a university publication that showed up in the mail was a highlight section about the "problem" professor. By the way the article was written you would have thought he had solved all of the world's children's health problems, and he didn't even want to research children. I was triggered. I was crying. I called my mom, and I was emotionally upset.

Around a month later, a spirituality center that I was attending was offering a forgiveness workshop. I had an awareness that this might help me with what was going on inside of me as a result of this graduate school experience. Prior to the workshop, I had started reading materials about the Center for Spiritual Living teachings, and I attended the Sunday gatherings. One of the primary teachings was that through the power of the mind, our thoughts, beliefs, and emotions, we create our reality. The books by Ernest Holmes, and the monthly Science of Mind magazine, resonated with me and were quickly opening me up and shifting my perception. I couldn't get enough of this life-altering content! I was primed and ready for what was coming in the workshop.

The workshop leader was awesome. She spoke, she sang, and right after the initial gathering, she led the workshop. She taught us that we are all born with core wounds and that we would experience events in life that would make us feel and experience these core wounds until we healed them. She suggested that we choose our parents too, and that if we have troubling experiences with our parents, they are a part of our healing journey. As long as we have our core wounds, we would continue to attract people and circumstances that are a match for our wounds. I was listening - and I was feeling it and getting it on a deep level.

Next she paired us with a partner to do an exercise where we talk to this person that hurt us. I can't remember all that we were supposed to say, but at the end I threw my arms around the woman who was my partner for the exercise. I thanked her and started laughing. I was feeling freer already!

For the last part of the workshop, we were instructed to now think of other times in our life, or other people that brought up the same stuff for us and had triggered our core wounds. Nothing came to me at that moment. But, that night when I was home and the kids were in bed, I was doing some reading and playing a song by the woman who led the workshop. All of a sudden I knew when I had experienced my core wounds in the past. It burst up inside of me and I cried hard…I cried a healing cry.

When I was six years old, a young man tricked my two little friends and me by telling us there were rabbits in the garage. I went in the garage and didn't see them. Then he told us that they were in the house. I followed him in, and my little girlfriends followed me. I trusted him and I shouldn't have. I blamed myself for getting my friends and I into this situation. The police caught the man that day, and I had to testify in court. My friends weren't emotionally able to testify, so I did and I had to do it on two separate occasions. It was a lot for a little girl to go through.

So, even though the experience in graduate school and the experience when I was six were different circumstances, I was able to connect with my soul and feel the connection of these events to my core wounds. A lot aligned for me to feel, heal, and release the emotional baggage I had been carrying. I knew I was not a victim of what had happened, but that from the level of my soul, I co-created it as a reflection of what my soul was carrying. This is the story of my shift in perception from victim to creator.

About a year after this forgiveness workshop, I was doing a past-life regression session with a facilitator. I brought up my experience with the graduate school advisor to see if there was anything related from a past-life. I don't recall all of the details, but what I "saw" during this regression was that my soul had shot his soul with an arrow during a battle. So for me, and my experience, I became aware of a karmic event that was showing up in this life. We can have awarenesses like this, but I feel we don't need to attach to the story of it. Just notice what you feel and see, and let it go.

We don't have to have hugely emotionally charged wounds in us that need all kinds of work. We may or may not have negative life experiences to take a look at. The important thing is to take notice as to how we are giving our power away. Is there something that you keep ruminating about, or is there continued drama in any of your relationships? The key in all of this is to own our emotions and to stop blaming other people for what comes up in us. Notice if you are finding yourself easily offended or triggered.

When we can feel our emotions and not make it about other people,
we start taking back our power and taking the charge off of the energetic connection with the other person.

The people who show up in our life and trigger us are reflections of us and where we have to do some healing. These reflections may show up in a boss, a friend, a lover, a parent, a spouse, or someone we don't know. Yet, the soul knows. The best question we can ask ourselves when we are in a difficult situation with another person is: what is this person reflecting for me? When we blame others for the emotional reactions rising up in us, think about how we are pointing a finger at them. When we point a finger at someone else, there are three fingers pointing back at ourselves. Try pointing your finger like you are pointing at someone else and notice how the middle finger, ring finger, and pinky are pointing back at you.

Point at someone else - and three fingers point back at you!

This is also significant when we judge people. If we are saying that someone is an idiot, for example, this is actually a reflection of how we feel about ourselves. This is part of our *shadow* that is so uncomfortable for us humans to feel within ourselves that we project it onto other people. When we perceive life in this way, we free others by no longer judging them, and we free ourselves by being able to notice what is going on inside of us.

Another way we free others is by assuming nothing and making no generalizations. It is often human nature to want to group people together, for instance, we make assumptions, we generalize, and we think we know a lot about people because they are Catholic, or because they are liberal, or because they have a high-level degree, or because they came here from another country. The problem is that in fact we know nothing about people as individuals, their values, why they do what they do, and why they feel the way that they do. On our end, being open minded to other views, and freeing ourselves from our own strong opinions and positions, liberates us. It takes self-awareness to observe ourselves, and to see where we are making generalizations and assumptions about people based on the box that we have put them in. Let go of this. See the Go(o)d in them that is the same stuff that is in you.

We also free others by not being demanding. And by this I mean when we accept, love, and feel supported by Life itself, we no longer seek and need love, support, and validation from others. Having expectations that others can't fill for you will always lead to disappointment. Shifting into feeling the unconditional Love and support of God makes it so we aren't being needy with other humans. When we are needy, our needs will never be met, because it can't come from other people.

Further, we can't truly receive true Love, until we love ourselves.

We have to first love ourselves
unconditionally in order to love others
unconditionally.
We free others by freeing ourselves.

Free others by using these recreators:
My relationships are light, loving, and fun.
I love unconditionally.
I am accepting and kind.
I see the Good in everyone I meet.
I listen with full presence.
I am open and accepting.
I am supported, honored, and respected - and I support, honor, and respect.
I speak my truth, and I am heard.
I release everyone to Love.
I love the world and the world loves me.
I let go and I let Love.

Chapter 7: Free Our Intuition

We all have the ability to be intuitive. At various times in my life, I have had very clear intuitive experiences of knowing something, knowing when someone was not telling the truth, or hearing a voice that guided me. However, I wasn't raised in an environment where that was a part of our everyday conversation. It wasn't a part of conversation with my friends either. I kept my intuitive experiences to myself. In fact, I didn't even know that it was called *intuition*. My intuition always came with an inner feeling of knowing that what I was getting was very true. I started to have more intuitive experiences during my spiritual awakening - and even more when I started meditating and doing other healing techniques to clear my energy field and get out of my lower-brain.

It has been my experience that the more we get out of our lower-brain stress and limited thinking, the more we tap into our connection to God, Life, the Universe, or whatever you want to call it, as well as our insight and intuition. There are also a lot of books that discuss this concept for tapping our own wisdom and creativity. FYI, I am being general when it comes to the science in this book, because I think there is more that we don't know than we actually do know. When it comes to the brain, science had at one time told us the brain didn't change once we were mature. However, now we know the brain is neuroplastic, that is, it is constantly changing and recreating itself. And remember how we were told that eating eggs was bad because of the cholesterol? Well, now we know that eggs are good for the body, and the story around cholesterol is changing. Further, for many years we have talked about our genes like what we get is what we get, however we are learning that our gene expression changes also. This is simply a reminder for us to be hesitant about what we attach to as *true*, and to maintain an open mind. Sometimes, we humans are letting our knowledge get in the way of our wisdom. When we are open-minded, we are able to feel or know what is true even if we don't yet know what the research would show. Research is awesome, and research has limitations. Okay, back to the book...

All of the great spiritual leaders teach that meditation helps to open our intuition, and I feel that living in a present meditative state throughout the day also supports this. We have a Higher path for ourselves, and we can be guided along the way. Life, God, the Universe, whatever you want to call it will show us the way. We have to be present and open to being guided by feeling, seeing the signs, and trusting. When we are able to tap into our intuition and peace, life gets a lightness about it and takes on a magical and easy expression. The more we start living in the present moment, the more we experience states of happiness, inner-peace, freedom, ease, and bliss. And, the more we experience these temporary states, the more they become our permanent traits.

We experience and sense with our intuition in different ways, and these pathways are called, clairvoyance (seeing), clairaudience (hearing), clairsentience (feeling), claircognizance (knowing), clairsalience (smelling), and clairgustance (tasting). We may have experiences with all of these, and some may show up as a more predominant way that we intuit. The more and more I live in the present moment, the more I have come to trust that I am exactly where I am supposed to be or meant to be in any moment. Urgency and angst dissolve and a greater freedom and purpose emerges. From this space, we can trust our intuition to guide us when we need it.

When my first born son started first grade, we found ourselves in a place that could have been very stressful. Thankfully, I had had enough Higher

Brain Living® sessions that I didn't regularly perceive life as stressful. However, there was still a lot of unknown and being uncomfortable with uncertainty was something I needed to heal. We had a purchase agreement on a house, and I started driving my first grader across three cities to the school by the house we thought was going to be ours in a month. The sellers and their realtor ended up canceling our purchase agreement in order to sell to someone they knew. So, we were on the hunt for another house, and I continued to drive my son to the new school, since the school year was underway. I was also driving my other little guy to a preschool on the way across town. I was spending two-to-three hours in the car everyday between three cities. Whew!

We started the school year expecting a month of the excessive driving, but by the time we found the right house and got to our closing date, it had turned into five months. One morning while driving to the school, I saw Ernie from Sesame Street in my intuitive vision (clairvoyance). I found it interesting, chuckled a little, and I had no idea what it meant. Later that day, as we were driving back home after school, I noticed an SUV in front of us with ERNIE on the license plate! Oh Hallelujah, I thought! For me, this was a message from God, the Universe, Life, my Higher Self,… whatever you want to call IT, that everything was Perfect. I rested into knowing that it was all going to be okay, and the house situation was working out the way it is meant to.

Another example of a clairvoyant experience of mine was during the school year when my youngest son had started kindergarten. While I was a bit sad that the toddler days with my littlest boy were over, I was very much excited about the opening and the freedom that would happen when both boys were in school. While I had clients through my business, and an intention to give myself some "me time" for the fall, I was feeling uncertain about what to "do" next.

One morning, I prayed to be guided to know what I was being called to next, and where to put my attention. That evening, I was in bed ready to go to sleep when I had a vision of a beautiful angel wing. I can't use words to describe this beautiful image, because there are no words. I was thinking "Wow, so beautiful," but I had no idea what it meant or why I was seeing it.

The next morning I was volunteering at my boys' school. I was sitting right outside the classroom correcting spelling tests when I overheard the teacher say "raise your wing...." to the kids, instead of raise your hand. This was guidance letting me know that I was right where I was meant to be, and was doing exactly what I was meant to be doing. I knew without a doubt that helping at the boys' school was a part of my Highest purpose during this time. The confirmation was helpful to me because sometimes I would wonder if I "should" be getting more clients or if I "should" get a faculty job and put my PhD into practice. (NOTE: dump your shoulds!) There truly is a part of us that "knows" and you absolutely can "follow your heart", as the saying goes.

Not only will our intuition let us know that we are on the right path,
it will also give us nudges into knowing and trusting what our body needs as well.

First and foremost, it is important to trust Life, and that whatever food is in front of us is okay for our body and it won't harm us. If there is something specific that would be beneficial, Life will lead us to it. Most often, we can go with what "sounds or feels" good to us. We have to give up thinking about food with restrictive thinking around choosing what we think we "should" eat or we "shouldn't" eat.

Here is an example of an experience of my intuitive guidance with food. I attended an energy healing workshop in Carmel, California one weekend and they had only two options on the menu each evening. On one of the days, I stopped into the grocery store and right away I noticed the eggplants stacked so nicely near the entrance. They struck me as so beautiful and so rich in color, and I also felt an intuitive feeling or knowing when I saw them. Since they had stood out to me during the day, when I saw the dinner choices (1) chicken parmesan or (2) eggplant parmesan, I chose the eggplant. Typically I was not very adventurous in trying new dishes, and because of my fitness background, I would have historically chosen the chicken dish because it was higher in protein. However, because the eggplant nudged me intuitively during the day, I decided to try the eggplant parmesan. Oh my, it was so delicious. I was not expecting it to be so satisfying, but I loved it. Yes, we can be guided and nudged into nourishing our bodies in a liberating way. Plus, being open and willing to flow this way just makes life so much more fun and magical.

Clairaudience is the intuition when we hear "something." It could be a variety of different sounds, or it could be a voice. I believe that an intuitive would make an awesome member on a health care team. I hope the future of healthcare moves into a more whole approach that includes mental, emotional, and energetic causes of disease. One day I was listening to a woman who was telling me about her health condition. She continued, saying that her father, who was a medical doctor, didn't believe that she had what she thought she had going on. As she was telling me this, I heard a voice say, "He's right." I was thinking, "Where did that come from?" And, "Oh yes, I get it." Hearing that voice helped me to clearly understand and know what was going on for the woman telling me about her health issue. Take note if you hear a guidance this way or even if a song pops into your head - it is significant.

Here's something to keep in check when it comes to intuition. For me, I simply trust life, and that if there is something I need to know, I will know it or I will be guided. I am not running around trying to read everyone - and crossing boundaries that I shouldn't. I once had someone who was an intuitive ask me something about a personal situation the moment she saw me - and I hadn't asked for her intuition on it. I felt that she was crossing a boundary and using her intuition inappropriately. Bottom line is, if you are intuitive, don't try to give people more than they are seeking. We want to let go of any need to try to prove ourselves.

My hope is that by my sharing these personal examples of how intuition has shown up in my life, you will begin to see or become more aware of how you are and have been guided in your life. In trusting our guidance, we can surrender to the Higher path that is wanting to unfold for us. If life is feeling hard or like a struggle, we may be resisting the natural flow and not living aligned with the God self part of ourselves. We don't have to figure everything out or live in doubt and worry.

Life guides us to the
extent that we pay attention,
notice the signs, and move
with Life instead of resisting it.

Here are some recreators for creating a guided life based in trust and certainty:

I know exactly what to do and when to do it.

I feel what is right for me, and I follow inspired action.

I trust my guidance.

I see clearly.

I know what I need to know when I need to know it.

I am insightful, intuitive, and wise.

I follow my signs from the Universe.

I trust Life.

Chapter 8: Free Our Children

Nobody ever told me parenting would be so demanding. It is quite a constant effort that has to happen, especially as a stay-at-home mom. When my children were little, I remember feeling like I simply needed to make it through the day. I just needed to survive until they went to bed. Then, once they were sleeping, thank goodness, I would be able to sit down and chill out. In general, I would say that my kids have been easy kids, but that doesn't mean that it has been easy. When I first starting reading some books by Ernest Holmes and learned about the power of the mind and that we can create ease in our lives from the inside out, I blissed out. I was so excited and so inspired that I would be able to free myself from the heaviness, like life weighing me down, that I had created around daily living. I was feeling like, "Oh yes, I'm listening. Sign me up!"

As a parent with two little ones, things that used to take me five minutes took fifteen minutes. I felt constantly distracted and interrupted, I could rarely focus on anything that took any amount of brain power if I was with my little ones. All that said, there is nothing like children to bring out and show you the love that is inside of you. I have felt more love and connection to all of life since I had my boys.

I took a position at the university when my second son was one year old. For me, it was much easier to get ready for the day, leave the house, and have someone else care for my kids. However, during this year's time, I learned that wasn't what I wanted for my family. I enjoyed "being" with my kids, I wanted to be their primary caregiver, and I didn't want to create a frantic, busy lifestyle for us. Fortunately, with the cost of child care and the priceless opportunity for me to raise our younglings, my husband agreed with my being a full-time mom. I believe that when we honor our values and make choices that may be hard or scary, yet we take a leap, Life will always support us in that. God doesn't want us to live an unfulfilling life, so sometimes we may have to take some leaps into a new direction that better serves our families and our own happiness.

There is nothing like kids to show us adults where we need healing. Our kids trigger us and bring stuff up in us that we didn't know existed. The important thing is to keep in perspective that it is not the children making us feel a certain way. It isn't their fault. Like I wrote about in Chapter 6, Free Others, the emotions that come up for us in parenting are ours. If we are feeling overwhelm, frustration, or short on patience inside or if we are blowing up and yelling at our kids, then we have some inner work to do.

Meditation is the most immediate thing we can do for healing right now. It requires nothing of us except to sit still. When we are living from a place of peace and stillness, we are better able to tune into the best next step for us and for our families. Investing in your own personal growth will do nothing but wonderful things for your family and you. Consider going deeper and investing in healing modalities and teachings that can reveal the True You, happy, fulfilled, at peace, and on purpose.

When we are living from a place of peace and stillness, we are better able to tune into the best next step
for us and for our families.

These days I ask myself whether what I am doing, or if I am taking time away from my family, serves the Highest Good for our family. When that is the guiding light, then everything falls into place perfectly and peacefully. My husband has been supportive of all of the changes I have made because he says, "I seem very happy." And that is true. As I have truly owned and healed my emotions, my triggers, and my mind, I have become much happier on the inside, I am a more present and joyful mother and wife. Now I have energy throughout the day instead of feeling tired, and I live more inspired and spontaneously without making things heavy or overwhelming. Moreover, I have much more clarity about what I keep on my plate so that I don't spread myself too thin.

Life changes when we are really present with our children - and I mean, completely present. I feel that cell phone over-use, drinking alcohol, and living very busy lifestyles have gotten in the way of real connection in our families. Several years ago, I was in Chicago at a training, and I decided to go out to dinner. I went by myself, sat at a booth, and ordered some food. The restaurant was very quiet and then a couple of families showed up and they were seated at tables close by and in my line of sight. Both of the families had a small child in a high chair and another older child. Both sets of parents had alcoholic beverages. I noticed one of the dads had a martini and then started drinking wine, sharing the bottle that his wife had ordered. The other family had the beer and wine flowing. I noticed there was a lot of cell phone use, and hardly any engagement between the couples or even with their children. It made me sad. And, I wondered, "Who is going to be driving home?" I was shocked that parents would drink and then drive with their precious cargo.

I enjoyed drinking before I had kids. But, kids brought on a demand to life that I had didn't want alcohol to play a part in. I knew that I couldn't be operating at 100 percent as a parent with alcohol in my life. The farther and farther I got away from alcohol, the less and less I wanted it. And the less I had, the more I felt its negative effects. As I was feeling more of my emotions instead of feeling numb, I became very aware of how alcohol numbed me for days after having only one glass of wine. Soon I lost my taste for it altogether.

Alcohol is a depressant, and this doesn't align with my desire to be a happy mom and functioning optimally. As I was learning more about expanding my consciousness, it was clear to me that alcohol would interfere with my growth. Because alcohol is a depressant, I don't want alcohol to limit my spiritual growth. Some research has suggested that one serving of alcohol per day is good for our cardiovascular system, however new research is showing that it has very detrimental effects on the brain.

I haven't drunk any alcohol since May of 2014, and I haven't missed it. In our society, it seems like a lot of adults don't know how to relax or have fun without it. Alcohol gets used to de-stress or escape. But, what if we didn't need to escape, and what if we didn't perceive life as stressful? What if we were so okay and comfortable in our own skin and in life in every moment that we didn't need alcohol to alter ourselves, to relax, or to have fun?

For my husband and me, parenting with alcohol simply isn't how we want to show up for our kids.

What if we didn't need to escape, and what if we didn't perceive life as stressful?

Let's talk about children a bit. From the time our babies are in our wombs and from birth and onward, our children are conditioned. And we adults have been conditioned in the same way. We take on the beliefs of society and our parents - we learn if we can trust others - we learn if it is safe to be seen or safe to be ourselves - we learn if we are bad or good - and we build a whole life around defending that. At very young ages, we decide if we are worthy, lovable, smart, and capable. As parents, we play such a significant role in creating a safe environment for our children to be themselves, to accept who they are, and to become all that they already are…. God-stuff.

As parents, we can ask ourselves:

- Are we encouraging our children to be their unique expression of their Godly self or are we causing our children to cover up their light?
- Do we allow them to be free, or are we causing them to protect themselves?
- Are we enabling them to tune into and trust themselves?

One of the deepest healings, that must happen to liberate ourselves is *to heal our shame*. This is a deep belief that we are "bad." We take this on as a toddler when we get in trouble, get scolded, and get icky shaming looks from our parents or other adults. If you let yourself feel deeply enough, uncovered by escapism, alcohol, drugs, television, work, or whatever, I will guarantee you that a bit of "I am bad" is in there. I didn't realize I had it in me until one day when I actually felt it. We have to feel it to heal it. So, the question becomes: how do we not shame our children? And yet, remember that our kids chose us, so they will learn from us what they need to learn from us. They are on their own journey, and as parents we have to let go sometimes and let them become who they are meant to be. That may be different from the ideas valued when we were raised.

We can prevent a lifetime of pain, confusion, or disconnection from their true selves for our kids, if we teach them that they are good, they are loved, and they are perfect just the way they are.

In helping to support our children to accept themselves and be grateful for who they are, we have to stop comparing them to their siblings. My husband and I watch the way that we talk about our kids. Our boys are so different and they need to be supported in different ways. I could go on and on about this and other ways they were and are different. It is important to know that one is not better than the other, and it is important to show our children that one way of being is not better than the other. I talk to my boys about how cool it is that they are beautifully unique and will grow into their own talents - and that is true for all kids. My husband and I do our best to not talk about them and compare them when we are with them. If as parents, we are comparing and contrasting our kids, it isn't honoring to their souls or to them as individuals. When they overhear the comparing, it may make them take on bad feelings toward themselves or make them overly competitive with their siblings and others.

If as parents, we aren't living from our own self-acceptance, inner-peace, contentment, and joy, how do we raise children who are? Are we being cognizant about what we are talking about around our children? How do we talk about other people around our children? And, if you don't have children, what are you speaking of around the children that are in your presence?

Teaching our children to accept, honor, and respect themselves and others, can only be taught by adults who accept, honor, and respect themselves and others.

You might be surprised to hear that I feel that one of the greatest factors in familial sanity and creating a harmonious household has to do with the family sleep patterns. For children, sleep is so important for growth, ability to learn, and emotional and behavioral development. In adults, lack of sleep has been compared to torture. If the parents find lack of sleep rough, think about how the baby or child feels - they are trying to grow, and learn, and adapt to the world. Any parent with a baby that is waking up at night will tell you that it makes for some tough times. When my boys were babies, even if they were waking one time a night, I felt like a zombie the next day. When I was pregnant with my first son, I had some friends with new babies. I was listening to them describe the multiple baby wakings night after night. I was thinking, "Oh my, heck no, I can't do that."

I decided I needed to learn about this sleep thing before my baby arrived. I picked up a book called, *Healthy Sleep Habits, Happy Child*, by Dr. Marc Weissbluth. I want to highlight some important concepts from this book, because adequate sleep is so foundational in creating emotionally balanced, happy, and easy-going kids. I feel that sleep is something that has to be honored and nurtured in our children from birth onward. Babies and little kiddos shouldn't have dark circles or bags under their eyes. A few important points from the book certainly drove how we honor our kids' need for sleep in our household.

Adequate sleep is so foundational in creating emotionally balanced,
happy, and easy-going kids.

First, I was so surprised when I read that babies *naturally and biologically* want to go to sleep at 5:30pm. For some reason this really struck me and I felt when I read it that, as a parent, I don't really want to mess with that. Another important point was that when babies yawn, you have a window of opportunity to get them to sleep, but by the third yawn that window is closing. If they miss the sleep window, then it will be more challenging for them to go to sleep. I noticed this yawn concept in my boys when they were babies. Sure enough, they told me when they needed to nap and when it was time for bed at night when they showed me their first yawn.

As infants, I flowed with my boys the first few weeks. Then over a short period their bedtime got earlier. By about two months of age, they went to sleep between 6-6:30pm every night. This early bedtime also held true for them for most of their days as toddlers. As a kindergartener, my son did best emotionally and behaviorally if he was asleep by 7-7:30pm. From a kid happiness standpoint, Dr. Weissbluth says that for babies, toddlers, and kids', *sleeping in doesn't make up for sleep lost due to too late of a bedtime*. And sleep begets sleep, so the earlier to bed, the more they will sleep. Further, he talks about how there is no such thing as separation anxiety. Lack of sleep and too late of bedtime makes infants and toddlers clingy.

My boys are early risers and are usually up by 6-6:30am. When we have tried later bedtimes, they would still get up at the same time. So, we have been pretty consistent with bedtimes. Being a full-time mom with them all day, I was very aware of how messing with their bedtime affected them the next day. It made my day with them not as fun, so early to bed it was. As a second grader, our older son stayed up a little later than his younger brother and he would read on his own while we got his brother to sleep. Then after reading, he would be asleep by 7:45-8:00pm.

I write about this in this book because I know that sleep is the single greatest factor - more than any other health type of activity - that contributes to a happy, healthy home. There has been more and more research reporting the benefits of sleep, and my hope is that more and more parents will start choosing consistent and early bedtimes for their children. But why wait for the research, when we can see the effects of too late of bedtime in our children.

Sleep is the single greatest factor - more than any other health type of activity - that contributes to a happy, healthy home.

Now in raising children who are living from their God self, I feel there is truth to the song lyrics, "I believe the children are our future. Teach them well and let them lead the way…." Remember that song by Whitney Houston? As a mom, the idea of letting them lead the way comes to my mind quite frequently, as I was a teenager who was spread too thin. I was in a lot of activities. In high school I worked at a grocery store, played sports, played three instruments in band, sang in two choirs, and I started teaching group fitness classes. I was burned out then, and I was burned out in college, graduate school, and in the early years as a mom. Growing up, my mom encouraged us to "be involved" because it was good for college applications. While I liked what I was doing, I think I did a little too much based on the motivation of being "good" and "building my resume."

When my kids were babies I remember thinking that I wanted them to be involved in music, sports, etc. But, I recall this one time when I was observing and thinking about my husband and his upbringing. He didn't play sports and he wasn't in the band, but he turned out so great. I was noticing how he loves his work, he played drums on his own in high school and as an adult, he puts his nice head on his pillow and falls right to sleep at night, and he wakes up and jumps out of bed in the morning to start the day. His motivation seems effortless, while my motivation used to feel so hard. I started to question whether all of the activities actually served me as a child and teenager. And these days, the demands on kids are so much more. Sports opportunities are starting at younger and younger ages and the time spent in these activities is becoming more and more.

Kids are starting all kinds of activities at a much younger age and with greater frequency. Many activities are happening in the evening instead of right after school. At least in the Twin Cities of Minnesota, parents are driving kids all around the area for their activities. When I was a kid, activities happened right after school at the school. The times are very different, and there is a "more is better" mentality - and thus the demands on the family have changed. Families are spending entire weekends chasing and traveling for sports, dance, etc. While I think it is important to support our children in fulfilling their dreams, I am not convinced that this is for the *Greatest Good* of our kids and our families if it is taking away from *family and free time.*

That said, I come back to the notion of "Let them lead the way." Perhaps we encourage and support what our kids express interest in. However, I think as parents, we have to check in with ourselves and make sure that the activities for the kids aren't *our way* of trying to fit in and/or our way of feeling valuable because we are busy. I was happy the day when my oldest son came home from first grade and said he wanted to learn how to play piano after seeing other kids playing piano at school. His little brother also wanted to play. I wasn't sure if maybe he was too young, but we let them start anyway. They share a 30-minute time slot with the teacher, and at home, I get to lead them and be with them on the piano. If they are enjoying it and are passionate, then I am happy to enable them. It is a balance between encouraging and allowing.

Pretty much every parent I have crossed paths with complains about the "busy schedule". One parent I knew seemed proud about her child's schedule, but usually I do not hear other parents say that they are loving their childrens' schedule. Perhaps as a whole, we are feeling that it may be *too much too soon*. I enjoy a generally open schedule for my boys. They have time to be creative, play, run around outside, and enjoy each other. They run out the door to play outside at every opportunity - cold weather or hot. As my kids are now elementary school-age, I wouldn't want to take that away from them.

So then, as parents, sports coordinators, dance program leaders, etc. *are we honoring our children*? Do we give them the space to figure out and feel who they truly are - free from all their activities and definitions?

Personally, I loved to read as a kid, and I lost that passion through rigorous academics. I didn't know what I was passionate about once I left high school, when the definitions I had of myself were stripped away. I had created a life of "doing" what I thought I "should" do, and I didn't know that it was *honoring my soul* to follow my heart, be creative, accept myself, and play. I moved through my undergraduate college years to go on to get my doctoral degree. I know that was my perfect path and journey. I have noticed in the world of adulthood that degrees don't determine happiness, success, or quality of character. I was 34 years old when I finally found my passion and my calling. I would love to see our children and young adults knowing themselves at a young age instead of having to struggle to figure it out later in adulthood.

I certainly don't have all the answers. I do know that when parents are living from the joy and Love of their Godly self, they create an environment where their children can, too. We are guided to a life of balance that honors our soul, our purpose, and our families, if we are open to it and we surrender to it. And, we can lead our children to live from their true radiance now.

Recreators for family contentment:
Being a Mom/Dad is so easy for me.
I know, see, and feel exactly what my children need.
Being a family is fun and joyful.
I am calm and peaceful.
My open heart leads the way.
I easily know and honor what is the Highest Good for my children.
I trust that everything is working out perfectly.
I am connected and loved.
I am grateful for my family.
I let God/Love/Life lead my parenting.
We Love.

Chapter 9: Free Our Godly Potential

How do you define potential? What does success mean to you? My definition of success has certainly changed over the years, and that has happened as I was becoming more and more clear about what I value. Eventually, I saw my potential as being beyond this material world and the acquiring and accomplishing. My Highest potential is becoming a clear vessel for the expression and transmission of Love in the world.

Before my spiritual awakening, I viewed my potential as growing up, getting my degrees, having a career, getting married, having children, getting a super cute dog, and having a home. I didn't see further beyond that. And I didn't have a life view much deeper than that. Something inside of me started questioning it. First, I started wondering why am I not waking up joyful and happy to start my day in the morning. I have everything I have every wanted. I had arrived at the place I considered as success. Soon after that, I started questioning my career in research. I remembered that even as a kid, I had wanted to help people. And while I could argue that I was helping people with my intervention research in pediatric health, I realized that *I wasn't* truly helping people. And as I became more aligned with my God self, I realized that I hadn't been helping anyone in a way that truly mattered. I had learned that helping people to live from their God self was the only meaningful way for me to really help people, since not living aligned with our God self is the only real problem.

For me, I discovered that the activities associated with research were somewhat self-promotion and approval-seeking focused, and not about helping people and really making a difference in the world. Regardless of where we work or how we go throughout our days, we all always have to remember to question why we do what we do. Is it purely motivated or are we trying to prove ourselves? Are we seeking approval? Or, are we just doing what we do because we think we "should?"

I had this realization about my academic career around the same time I was figuring out that I didn't want to take myself away from my family to continue on this career path. Ultimately, what I discovered was that if I did want to help other people, then I needed to help myself first. I knew if I did want to serve my family in a valuable way, I needed to take a look at what was going on inside of me. This is where my healing journey began.

Eventually, I learned that the only person I really need to help is myself. The more I heal myself, the more I heal the world, because the world is us. The more I am content, peaceful, and happy on the inside, the more I can give to others.

Remember the saying, "If momma ain't happy, ain't nobody happy."? First, I had to feel alive enough to truly support my family, and only then could I really begin to feel alive enough to serve beyond my family. I couldn't support others until I felt supported. But, I had to realize that support doesn't come from other people. We think we want to be supported by others, yet we can't feel supported by others until we are feeling supported by Life Itself. True support must come from the inside. This is an energetic experience. It is a journey of Self-discovery. It is a journey of realizing the everything is within us.

We can't feel supported by others
until we are feeling supported by Life Itself.

I feel that the greatest determinant of a person who realizes any kind of potential is the belief that he/she "can." Henry Ford said, "Whether you believe you can or you can't, you're right." That is true. I have often wondered about *the cans and the can'ts*. I've always believed that I can, and I take steps in that direction. My sin was that I made everything weigh on me, and this made things harder than they needed to be. I am not smarter or better than anyone - I've simply believed that I could do something, and I did it. If I can do it, you can do it, and if any human can do it, you can do it. If you have no desire to do it, then it isn't yours to do.

Ask yourself:
- Do you limit your potential by comparing yourself to others or thinking you have to compete?
- Do you ever *not do something* because you think you could not do it as well as someone else or because you won't be perfect?
- Are you all-or-nothing, so if you think that you could never do a marathon then you simply won't even run? (I am not advocating marathons here, but it's an extreme example of all-or-nothing thinking.)

- Is there anything that you are you telling yourself you can't do? For example, "I can't meditate," "I can't do yoga," "I can't get into graduate school," or "I can't dance."

I used to think that my workout had to be an hour, and if I didn't have that kind of time then I didn't move my body. Why didn't I just go outside and enjoy a thirty-minute stroll? Because,.... I had insane thinking.

Most of us are operating from some sort of insanity that is preventing us from true happiness, fulfillment, and our unique potential.

So, if our true potential is to be and radiate all of the God-stuff that we actually are, how does that show up as success, potential, or abundance in our lives? A potential exists within each and everyone of us that is so much greater than what we are currently expressing. What keeps us from moving forward in life? Many people feel there is something more to life than just trying to survive the day. What stops us from feeling the bubbling up of passion, aliveness, and Grace that is dying to be realized within us? Is it shame? Is it guilt? Is it fear?

All of us have a potential within us that is the same. That potential is Love, God, Life, whatever you want to call it. That potential is the same in you as it is in me and as it is in everyone in the world. We each have a unique expression of our potential that we can express, if we choose to. We may already be living what we know is our purpose, doing the work in the world that we were meant to do, but are we perceiving it as that? When I was facilitating Higher Brain Living® sessions, I had a client who was always complaining about his job. After several sessions, his perception shifted and he realized that he actually liked his job. He started approaching his work and talking about it with a lighter positivity. Also, one of the people he didn't enjoy at his work quit. When we change, the circumstances around us change.

As we transform and shift
the vibration of our energy,
what we attract to us also changes.

It's important to realize that when it comes to our potential - there is enough for everyone, and there's no such thing as competition. If you are feeling like you have to compete against others, then consider letting that go and trust that you are on your perfect path and they are on their perfect path.

We can all be successful,
fully living our potential,
and serving the people
we are meant to serve.

Now, if we clear out all of the mental, emotional, and energetic junk that is blocking us from fully expressing the joy, love, and freedom that is the radiance of the God within us, then our potential is alive and free in the world. From this vantage point, life becomes a light, magical, and fun experience instead of the worry, struggle, and limitation that humans are used to creating. From this clear, open space, *we attract our perfect path,* instead of thinking we have to figure it out or find it. Life is always a perfect reflection and unfolding, and we can start creating a more lovely, fun, and abundant life.

Anything we desire has in it a deeper reflection of the qualities of God that we desire. If we desire more world travel, then the essence of our desire may actually be freedom. We don't know how or when the world travel will show up and in what order, or where exactly we may go, but as we become more free on the inside, the better we will be able to attract or manifest an outward expression of freedom. If we have a wound in us that believes it isn't safe to be ourselves, it will prevent us from feeling very free on the inside.

As we heal those places inside,
emotionally or mentally,
that aren't free and don't feel safe,
then we create more freedom
in our experience.

When it comes to abundance, many people would love to create more abundance in the form of financial freedom. We limit ourselves by our beliefs about money or our limited thinking in how money can come to us. First of all, if we want more financial abundance, we can't be judging people who have money. If we are making it "wrong" to have money, then money, energetically, isn't going to be very attracted us. There is nothing wrong with money. I've heard Sandra Yancey, the founder of eWomenNetwork, say it this way, "Good people, who make good money, do good things." And a mindset that changed for me was that, "The more money you have, the more you can give." We have to let go of constructs that it is greedy to have money. While some people may be focused on money for material reasons or feel that their value is defined by how much money they have - you don't have to let that drive you. However, let go of concepts that you shouldn't dream of greater financial freedom because of greed. Let's open to our unlimited and infinite resources. God is the infinite source of our supply.

We must also look at the belief that making money is "hard." Saying things like money doesn't grow on trees, making it wrong to have money served on a silver platter, or beliefs that money only comes from "hard" work, energetically pushes money away from us. Do you want to create a life where money is hard and can only come to you through an hourly wage? Or do you want to create a life that feels light and inspired, and money and resources come to you easily? Also, take a look at how you feel about other people's financial success. Do you wish the same success, happiness, and abundance for everyone else that you wish for yourself and your family? If you notice some jealousy or envy in you, you may be energetically pushing money away.

I did an excellent online money mastery class led by a woman, and she taught that money is a reflection of our beliefs about ourselves. During one of the exercises, I was able to notice that my money pattern felt like there was *never enough* money. Further into the exercise, I tuned into that I didn't feel that *I was enough*. Woah! Really? Yep, our beliefs about ourselves are reflected in our finances. I was able to feel that so clearly. I had to shift my perception of myself into knowing that I am more than enough. I am plentiful! And you are, and always have been enough. Can you notice a pattern in your finances that reflects how you have felt about yourself?

Recently someone questioned me about how I described my business - as helping people shift into living in bliss and freedom. She suggested that I say something else that seemed more attainable. She thought that people might feel that it is "woo woo" or not possible. Do you believe that happiness is possible? I think that is the one true human desire - that all people want to be happy. We may think that accomplishing or getting things will make us happy, but ultimately it is not about external things. It is an inner experience. Yes, happiness, inner-peace, joy, contentment, ease, freedom, and even bliss is attainable. The research on consciousness and the brain supports this also. Changes in our brain correlate with our capacity to tune into, experience, and live our connection to God. Further, all the great realizers, saints, mystics, and sages have told us that our experience of God is indescribable bliss along with a great inner-peace and unconditional Love throughout our daily life. If you'd like to read the research, check out the neuroscience research by Dr. Andrew Newberg. He also has a couple of great books that summarize the God-and-brain research to date: *How God Changes Your Brain* and *How Enlightenment Changes Your Brain*.

Do we need someone else's proof? Why not simply try it out for yourself? I know that my life has been made anew. Change your thinking, heal your energy field, free yourself, in the present moment, always and forever, you are Infinite! Lighten, love, and be Free!

Try out some of these recreators for creating and living your limitless Godly potential:
I am guided to my Greatest Good.
I live my purpose in every moment.
Who I am is always enough.
I serve the world with my gifts.

I live my life on purpose in every moment.

I easily express my Godly potential.

My Highest path is crystal clear.

I am loved and supported by God.

God is the infinite source of my supply.

I am passionate about my work in the world.

I am the Love that God Is.

I live in bliss and freedom.

Money flows to me, and I gratefully receive it.

I am infinitely abundant.

I am financially free.

Chapter 10: Living Radiantly Free

Every problem we think we have
is simply to show us that it is an area in
which we are not living from our Godly self.

There is only one true problem and one true goal. Every problem we think we have is simply to show us that it is an area in which we are not living from our Godly self. All drama, chaos, and difficulty that shows up *for us* is reflecting to us what it is that we have created. In owning all aspects of ourself and our life, we can let go of projecting it onto others, and start seeing how we have co-created whatever it is that is showing up. I like how one of my friends has said it: "Who is the common denominator to all of your problems?"

The radiance of our God self is the following: unconditional Love, balance, harmony, joy, abundance, genius, health, light, clarity, peace, ease, and acceptance. Whenever there is something we are experiencing that isn't feeling like God-stuff, then we know we have some inner-healing to do. We create our heaven and we create our hell. And, once we know this, the choice is now ours.

We can take any goal we have and correlate that goal with an aspect of our Godly self we would like to reveal. So if we are continually experiencing financial lack, we may have a goal of finding a better paying job. Yet, the true goal in this is to live the abundance that God is. Scarcity and lack are frames of mind. When we see how blessed we truly are, we change our beliefs about life and abundance, then we begin experiencing our abundance showing up for us. God is the true source of our supply and it comes from aligning with our God-self.

If our goal is to have loving and supportive relationships, the true goal in that would be to experience and live the Love and support of God. We can't truly know love and support from others, because true love and support doesn't come from other people. To liberate ourselves from needing love and support from others, we must know and feel the Love and support of Life Itself. Further, if we aren't experiencing love and support from others, (1) we may not be giving it to ourselves first, and (2) it may be a reflection to us that we are not being loving and supportive to others. We will feel true Love and support when we stop needing support, love, or approval from others.

Living *Radiantly Free* is living lightly. We don't have to live in the heaviness, negativity, and overwhelm that is so pervasive in the world. Our freedom is right here waiting for us to claim it. Choose you, and choose happiness. The more we appreciate and revel in the beauty that is all around us, the more we take our focus off of perceiving things negatively and feel what a miracle it is that we are even here at all. When we bring our attention to the gratitude that we are alive and here at all, the heaviness that we have created around our drama and our story will lessen. You may experience some moments of overwhelm when you really understand that you are creating your experience. Feel it and decide to lighten up. In a short time, we will let go of the ways we used to drag ourselves down and begin being able to chuckle at the things that are showing up, in experience, in relationships, and in our own mind.

Whether we make life hard and heavy or light and fun is up to us. Perhaps we need to stop believing that for anything to be worth having, it has to be hard work. What if it doesn't have to be hard work? What if that is simply a perception we have created in our neuropathways in our brain. We have created the neuropathways in our brain to perceive and react to life in a certain way, and we can recreate our neuropathways to perceive and live in the way we really dream of.

My experience of choosing and shifting into being *Radiantly Free* has been so rewarding and so worth it. Over time, with more clarity, you see how the world is reflecting you, and your emotional charges diminish. You can see what you have created, and even laugh about it. There is no nobler path than in choosing to become *Radiantly Free*. When you heal yourself, you heal those around you. Your radiance ripples out into world. We heal the world by living from our God self. We can create our Heaven on Earth.

If you choose to become *Radiantly Free*, you may sense things, and you are also likely to experience life changes. Energetically, you may begin to feel your own vibration more and more. Sometimes this energetic shifting may make you feel slightly nauseous, tired, and out-of-it. There may be times when honoring yourself means you go to bed very early, and there may be times when you are quite restless, feeling very awake and aware, and unable to sleep. You may experience headaches or other aches and pains in your body. As you are shifting your energy and your emotions, this blocked energy will show up in your body. Your body is trying to heal itself. Trust and listen to your own body.

You may experience other sensations, such as a pressure or tingling sensation at the crown chakra/ skull area opening on the top of your head. You will feel if other openings are happening in your other chakra energy centers. You may experience coughing, unrelated to a cold or sickness, that is clearing your heart and throat chakras. You may also feel a pressure in the third eye chakra area of your forehead.

When it comes to food, you may find that foods you used to like no longer interest you, and there may be foods you need through various periods. Be aware of this attraction to various foods, and let it be okay. In general, you may find less interest in highly processed food. And yet, realize that this is not about determining that foods are harmful to you. You can listen to your body and allow it what it wants without becoming fearful or overly restrictive around food. Your body may need to purge, so you may experience flu-like symptoms, such as diarrhea and vomiting. It may not be about being "sick," simply allow this energetic shifting. Of course, consult a medical doctor if needed.

Let your body feel safe and open
in the world
and you will heal your body
and create a robust physiology.

My personal experience was that my body needed more rest. I was working out hard for years, but I began to follow my body, and I knew I had to trust it. I have taken more walks in the last two years than I had in my whole life. I also became less interested in having music playing during my physical activities. I now walk without music and I don't like the loud music in group fitness classes. I used to love to escape through music. Your preferences may change, and that is okay. We can follow our feelings and intuition from within us. I became more in tune with the way my body was protecting me and keeping me safe, rather than making my body weight about diet and exercise.

Start with a clean slate and clear all beliefs and rules you have for your body.
There is no reason we can't be radiantly healthy and happy in our bodies.

I also lost interest in alcohol or being in bar settings. I have become very content with a more quiet and peaceful lifestyle. At times you are called out into the world, and other times it may be best to slow down and have more time for silence and inner-listening. Our energy is moving toward being much more energy-efficient. Too much exercise may be wasting our energy, and there may be a better type of movement for our body. What our body needs may change over time, so it is best to not be too attached to only one form of movement. Stay tuned to the cues from the universe and the little nudges within you that let you know what may feel best. I was called away from the gym. I used to love the gym but now I either walk, dance at home, or go to our small community center gym for a quick in and out workout.

We may be called in other directions too. Perhaps we are meant to move to a higher vibration area, or even a lower vibration area that needs your presence. We may become interested in lightening our load and clearing our home spaces. If you have always worn a lot of black or tan, you may be drawn to more vibrant colors in your wardrobe. Your style may change. You may be less interested in trying to fit in - and be more willing to stand out and be seen. If you have always had the same hairstyle or hair color, you might find yourself ready for a change.

The descriptor, be "authentic," is heard a lot these days. To be truly authentic, there is no more hurt and no more feeling offended. If someone says something mean, critical, or sarcastic, you don't feel bad about it. You will find that you don't get offended anymore. A true confidence emerges in that you are absolutely okay with yourself in any moment, free from what you think anyone might think, and free from any self-criticism. More and more, fear diminishes. I think that people in general don't realize how afraid they are. If we play it safe, then we create a status-quo life. At a certain point, we may ask ourselves: Is there more than this? Yes, there is and always has been. It has always been within you to truly liberate yourself, your brilliance, your purpose, and to reveal who you truly are.

This doesn't mean you have to run out and save the world, and yet maybe you will. My experience was that I was called home for a while. I found myself called more and more to clear my schedule and create a family lifestyle, instead of a parent tag-team lifestyle. It took a bit for me to get comfortable and not think that I should be someplace else, whether that was working out, attending more personal growth classes, or volunteering my time. As I became more in tune with me, these decisions became quite clear, and I didn't need an explanation or understanding to why I was making these decisions. Life was living me the more that I would allow it and create the space for something new. You can trust the Life in you and trust your flow throughout the day.

At some point, a surrendering must happen for greater growth. Author Marianne Williamson said, "May God's Will Be Done, Not My Own." I had used those words as a mantra for a while when I would feel like there was something bigger to step into and I was feeling angst about the unknown. This was powerful for me in letting go of my agenda, and to live the life that is greater, beyond, and within me. What is wanting to be expressed through you?

Great power exists in being able to look at what your life looks like, and see that you've created this, and now, you can create something new.

A greater awareness emerges as we allow it, and we practice letting go of all of our small stuff. There are tools to speed up the process and facilitate our becoming *Radiantly Free*. Here are my personal favorites:

1. <u>Meditation</u> - build up to 20 minutes per day. More is fine, simply trust what you are being called to be. In my app, available for free in the Apple and Android stores, you can use the Time to Be timer for your meditation. It is

designed for silent meditation and you can set the timer for 1-60 minutes.

2. Silence - find time, at home after kids are in bed or while you are driving alone in the car, for silence. Turn off the music, turn off the television, and take some time throughout the day to feel and know you.

3. Powerful Mind - Don't forget that your mind, with all of your thoughts and beliefs, is very powerful. Change your mind to change your life. Notice your beliefs and what life is showing you and start telling yourself a new story. You can use the Recreators and Power Words in my app to pour something new into yourself and override your usual programming.

4. Higher Brain Living® & Source Code Meditation - this is an amazing program for rapid transformation. The technique shifts energy into the Higher Brian structures, thus

dumping lower brain stress and habits, and energizing the parts of our brain the tune us into our peace, insight, clarity, and bliss. Certified facilitators can take you through the program and/or retreats. Check this out. The sessions are so amazing. It is very revolutionary to be able to liberate our energy and move it into the brain, as has been shown with electroencephalogram measurements, and is done with this technique.

5. <u>Other modes for healing, alignment, and wellness</u> - You don't have to wait until you are sick to start taking care of your energy field and your body. Regular chiropractic, energy healing, acupuncture, massage, muscle testing for wellness, and learning can truly heal you from the inside out.

6. <u>Dance</u> - Dancing has been shown to have profound effects on the brain. Moving our bodies in an intuitive and free way is how our

bodies really want to move in order to heal, open, and release stress. Whether you need to dance freely at home in order to feel safe, or you want to find a dance community, start to let go of the rigidity in your body and let your body move in your own unique and beautiful way.

7. <u>Pause, breathe, and bring your awareness to the present moment</u>. It is easier to see, feel, and know our intuitive guidance when we are fully present.

Great power exists in being able to look at your life and see that you've created this, and now, you can create something new.

- Have you stopped dreaming bigger or having a vision for your life?
- Are you living in apathy and just trying to get through the day?
- Are you tired of problems and drama?
- Have you had enough of the "shoulds" of society that haven't led you to happiness?

- Did you stop expressing your needs because you don't want to rock the boat?

You can be free.

I am telling you that it is possible.

You can honor yourself and you can

honor others in a deep and profound way

by becoming all that you already are

and all that you are meant to be.

Let go of all extrinsic motivation. Let Life move you. You don't have to do it alone. The entire Universe is supporting you and moving you forward. We can create with it *or* we can resist it. Let's be light and take life lightly. Let go and let Love. We can create a world that works for everyone, and we start with ourselves. The more we dig into ourselves, the more the world shows up loving to us. A Divine spark exists within all of us, waiting for us to unleash it into a flaming fire.

This fire is the power that is all life, and it is the same Life in and through everything. There is gentleness and Grace in this fire. It is bubbling up in us and it is ready to flow.

Let's fly together!

Let's bliss together!

Let's be alive, well,

and free in the world!

Would you like Rachel's support for your inner-healing and growth in radiance?

1. Go to **www.drrachelw.com** to sign up for my newsletter!
2. Go to **www.rachelapp.com** to download my app!

Inside the Rachel app you will find the Time to Be timer for silent meditation. Connect with me, read my blog, and use the Time to Be meditation timer to heal your mind, body, and energy in order to become the Love that you truly are.

If you want more features for growth, healing, and recreating, Subscribe!

Tap on Power Words to get 1 of 53 randomly generated, but perfectly synchronistic, words to use during your meditation, as a mantra throughout the day, or as guidance or growth reminders.

Check out the the daily Recreator for teachings about healing or an affirmative statement you can say to guide you in aligning with your Godly potential and recreating your life into Love.

And, receive occasional Push notifications with quotes, reminders, and personal messages from me to support you on your journey.

Recreate, enlighten, and increase your vibration through my app!

In Love & Bliss,
Rachel

About Rev. Dr. Rachel Wetzsteon

Rev. Dr. Rachel Wetzsteon would have never guessed that she would have become a Reverend and wrote a book about spirituality and God. She experienced what is often called a *spiritual awakening* that shifted her into happiness and lightness, and drastically changed her perception of life and Truth. Her training in energy healing and teachings about the power of the mind in creating our lives changed her life dramatically. This awareness gave her a new context about God and the powerful way we co-create our experience and our world.

Rachel has an extensive background in the health industry and in health research. She has a doctoral degree in exercise physiology from the University of Minnesota and she has published numerous research articles. After teaching group fitness classes for 18 years, she realized she wasn't listening to her body and that there is a more loving way to honor her body and her energy. Rachel became attuned to the mental, emotional, and energetic aspects of our being.

After having children and experiencing changes in her values, she realized she wanted to help people in a more meaningful and powerful way. She awakened to living from the knowing, intuition, peace, and bliss of who she really is and a conviction that this is the only way to truly thrive.

Rachel now leads others to be the radiant light of who they truly are by supporting others' growth in radiance through her app (www.rachelapp.com) and her podcast, REV with Rachel, where the REV is Recreate ~ Enlighten ~ Vibrate, available on iTunes.

Books Mentioned in the Book

1. Brennan, Barbara A. (1987). Hands of Light: A Guide to Healing Through the Human Energy Field. New York, New York. Bantam Books.

2. Peirce, Penney. (2009). Frequency: The Power of Personal Vibration. New York, New York. Atria Books / Beyond Words Publishing, Inc.

3. Tolle, Eckhart. (1999). The Power of Now: A Guide to Spiritual Enlightenment. Vancouver, B.C., Canada. Namaste Publishing.

4. Chopra, Deepak, & Tanzi, Rudolph. (2012). Super Brain: Unleashing the explosive power of your mind to maximize health, happiness, and spiritual well-being. New York, New York. Random House, Inc.

5. Weissbluth, Marc. (2015) Healthy Sleep Habits, Happy Child. New York, New York. Ballantine Books/Random House, Inc.

www.ingramcontent.com/pod-product-compliance
Lightning Source LLC
Chambersburg PA
CBHW071219090426
42736CB00014B/2894